GW00758811

The Buildings of Georgian Lancaster

Andrew White

Centre for North-West Regional Studies
University of Lancaster

1992

General Editor: Oliver M. Westall

The Buildings of Georgian Lancaster

Andrew White

The Buildings of Georgian Lancaster

by Andrew White

This volume is the twenty-fifth in a series published by the Centre for North-West Regional Studies at the University of Lancaster. Details of other titles in the series which are available may be found at the back of this volume.

ISSN 0308–4310

Copyright © Andrew White, 1992

First edition, 1992

Published by the Centre for North-West Regional Studies, University of Lancaster
Designed and typeset by Carnegie Publishing Ltd., 18 Maynard Street, Preston
Printed and bound in the UK by Cambridge University Press, Cambridge

British Library Cataloguing-in-Publication Data
A CIP catalogue record for this book is available from the British Library

ISBN 0-901800-12-0

All rights reserved
No part of this publication may be reproduced, stored in a retrieval system, or transmitted in any form or by any means mechanical, electronic, photocopying, recording or otherwise, without the prior permission of the publisher.

Table of Contents

Acknowledgements iv

Introduction 1

- Stone Sources 3
- Architects 6
- Masons and Craftsmen 8
- Style and Design 10
- Services 15
- Gardens and Summer-Houses 15
- Poorer Houses 17
- Where did the money come from? 18
- New Developments 18

Gazetteer of Georgian Buildings 31

- Cable Street 31
- Lancaster Castle 32
- Lancaster Priory Church 32
- Castle Hill 32
- Castle Park 34
- Chapel Street 34
- Church Street 36
- Dalton Square 38
- Fenton Street 38
- Great John Street 41
- High Street 41
- King Street 42
- Market Square 43
- Market Street 43
- Meeting House Lane 43
- Moor Lane 43
- New Street 45
- Queen's Square 46
- Queen Street 47
- St. George's Quay 47
- St. Leonardgate 48
- Sun Street 49
- Water Street 50
- Outlying Buildings 50
- Skerton 53

Notes 54

Acknowledgements

I would like to thank a number of people for their help in putting this book together. My greatest debt of gratitude is to John Champness for advice, information and useful discussions. Jonathan Ratter and Stephen Gardner also lent some of their first-rate first-hand knowledge of the buildings, and the latter also provided a number of building plans. My colleagues Susan Ashworth, Paul Thompson and Wendy Moore respectively read the text and provided graphic and other help. At Lancaster Town Hall John Lee gave me access to deeds and unravelled the complexity of their filing while at Lancaster Central Library Isobel Gaddes and Susan Wilson uncomplainingly found, fetched and carried piles of manuscripts. Finally Katrina Hunter, Sandra Wilkinson and Helen Griffiths typed innumerable versions of my text.

All illustrations are from the collections of Lancaster City Museums unless otherwise credited.

Introduction

The Georgian buildings of Lancaster have not received the attention they deserve.

A long vernacular tradition of sturdy building, enhanced by the qualities of Lancaster stone, a short period of prosperity at a time of general good taste and a slump in the 19th century have left Lancaster with an exceptional range of houses and public buildings of the 18th and early 19th century. The abiding memory of Lancaster is of a Georgian town.[1]

Prosperity came with the growth of port trade in the mid-18th century, although a rebuilding boom had started somewhat earlier, changing Lancaster from a town of timber and thatch to one of stone. The establishment of St. George's Quay in 1750–5 and the New Quay in 1767 materially assisted the handling of goods. New warehouses and splendid Custom House set the seal on trading success, which brought the produce of the West Indies and of the Baltic through the port of Lancaster.[2] The outward and visible sign of prosperity was the quantity and quality of public and private rebuilding.

The trading success coincided with a

'South View of Lancaster', an engraving by Woolnoth after Farington, 1816. To an extent which has been almost forgotten, Lancaster was regarded in the 18th and early 19th century as a picturesque place in its own right, as well as being the natural stopping place for travellers to the Lake District. Its dignified architecture, attractive stone, and views towards Ingleborough and Morecambe Bay contributed to this in no small measure.

developing social calendar, hingeing on the Assizes, held twice each year in the Castle, and the Races, held on the Marsh. The atmosphere of the Assizes in the 19th century is admirably conveyed by Thomas de Quincey in his essay 'The English Mail-Coach',[3] where he describes the flood of lawyers and gentry into town on these occasions. Sir George Head, writing in 1835, also gives a flavour of the atmosphere;[4]

> 'The Assizes were unluckily on that very day at their zenith: a festival, of which the signs and phenomena below stairs, and in the streets, were apparent; – bloated country coachmen, in their best liveries, stood lounging in the stable-yards and gateways; every servant in the house jostled and trod on the heels of his fellow; dinner tables were laid in all the parlours; sand, in preparation for the scuffle, was spread on the floor instead of carpets; the lawyers ran to and fro in their wigs, and a group of hungry farmers in the passage, all panting and eager for the fray, whetted their large teeth, and licked their lips, as they snuffed up the sweet savour, or fragrant odour, from the kitchen . . .'

Nos. 76 (right) and (left) 80 Church Street, town houses respectively of the Marton family and the Wilsons of Dallam Tower. No. 76 is an older house refronted in the 1730s or 1740s and has extensive oak panelling, while 80 was built in 1772–5 and contains fine mahogany doors.

This description is almost certainly applicable also to the previous century.

It became fashionable for landed society to entertain during the Assizes and so a number of the minor nobility and gentry built town houses for this purpose. Amongst these were Dr. Daniel Wilson of Dallam Tower near Milnthorpe, Mr. John Fenton Cawthorne MP of Wyreside Hall, Dr. Oliver Marton of Capernwray, and the Duke of Hamilton, whose country house was Ashton Hall, three miles to the south-west. Many of these houses, and those of the new occupants of Dalton Square etc., were designed for entertaining, with large public rooms and consequent domestic economies. Many town houses had their principal rooms on the first floor.

The prosperity attracted able architects such as Thomas Harrison and J. M. Gandy. For the first time the public purse, in the form of the County or the Corporation, was able to pay for new public buildings, the latter by borrowing, from the sale of investments and from the growing receipts from the sale and lease of land for private building.

After 1800 the pace slackened; the wars with France cost a high price in lives, ships and cargoes lost to privateers. By 1820 the prosperity was largely at an end. It saved the inheritance of Georgian architecture because there was little money to rebuild. Not everything survives of course, but Victorian Lancaster was a very different place with different values and aspirations. It was content, in most cases, to subdivide and alter existing buildings rather than to demolish and rebuild. Of course most of the older streets contain some Victorian buildings and the textile mills lining the canal were a new and substantial feature of the town after 1800.[5]

There are many reasons for the collapse of prosperity. The movement of trade to Liverpool and the slump following the Napoleonic wars affected Lancaster badly. So did the slackening of trade with the West Indies. However, the failure of the town's two banks within a few years of each other in the 1820s destroyed much of Lancaster's credit and liquidity. It is computed that £420,000 at the prices of the day was lost in the two failures, and that was almost entirely borne by citizens of Lancaster. Some of it was paid back in due course, but the town took a long time to recover.[6]

Investment of savings at that time, before the coming of the railways, was a very localised activity and the consequences of bank failures were felt most keenly in a very small area. It is unlikely that anyone in Lancaster had much money to spare for building during the 1830s and 1840s and so the new buildings of this period are such churches as St. Thomas', the railway stations and the Oddfellows' Hall, all dependent upon the finances of a wider area.

Whatever the causes of Lancaster's economic decline the effect is that there was little money about to rebuild, extend or demolish older buildings after about 1820. As a result we have a very fine legacy of Georgian buildings, including virtually the whole of the 18th century quayside, to enjoy and cherish for the future.

Stone Sources

Lancaster is fortunate in having a wide variety of building stone, suitable for different purposes, available within a short distance. For exterior walling flush-jointed ashlar blocks were readily available. Many specifications called for 'polished freestone' which in effect meant the local sandstone rubbed to a flat finish, leaving no tooling marks. Such freestone came from

Some examples of stone-dressing using Lancaster stone. *Clockwise*: 4 Queen Street, *c*.1770, ('polished freestone' with lightly feathered borders); 5/7 Queen Street, *c*.1770, (false rusticated jointing in very large blocks); Shire Hall, *c*.1788, (punch dressed); Girls' National School, High Street, 1820, (horizontally broached and bordered).

Lancaster Moor, especially 'Windmill Hill' or 'Knotts' – there were up to seven separate quarries on the Moor during the 18th century. Another source was 'Mr George Gibson's Quarry near the Greaves in Scotforth'.[7] This was probably on the site of the present Brunton House.

Contemporary descriptions and recently-cleaned buildings suggest that the stone was almost white when fresh. However, where it has not been blackened by smoke the stone has generally weathered to a honey colour, with brownish streaks caused by iron impurities. That these were an original feature of the stone is borne out by the description of an anonymous Nottinghamshire visitor to Lancaster in 1764.[8] Of the new Custom House he says;

> '. . . a very handsome new building with a neat portico facing the river supported by four plain pillars, each formed of a single stone, beautifully veined . . .'

The Moor quarries and that at Scotforth now show no exposed faces. The latter seems to have been built over, while the former quarry rights on the Moor were bought out and the area landscaped in the 1870s and 1880s to form Williamson Park.

These freestone sources belong to the Namurian gritstone series. Another source, where exposed faces can still be seen, was at Damasgill or Mainstones Quarry in Ellel, seven miles south of Lancaster. The particular benefits of this stone seem to have been that it could be worked in very large blocks and that it had good water-resisting qualities. It was used for the monolithic columns of the Custom House in 1762–3, possibly for the columns of the Assembly Room (after 1759) and for the massive sections of the columns of the Old Town Hall of 1782–3. At Glasson Dock it was specified for the dock walls by the Port Commissioners in 1787.[9]

A description of 1820[10] characterises the stone thus:

> '. . . being of a peculiar nature not subject to decay, of a coarse but solid texture, free from those deceitful seams which too much of this country freestone abounds with.'

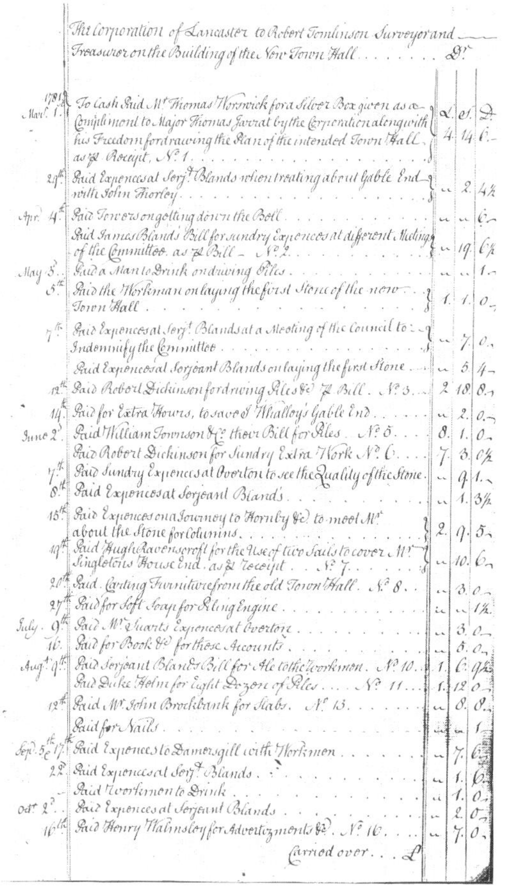

The Corporation of Lancaster to Robert Tomlinson Surveyor and Treasurer on the Building of the New Town Hall . . . . Dr.

		£	s	D
1781 Mar. 1.	To Cash Paid Mr Thomas Worswick for a Silver Box given as a Compliment to Major Thomas Jarrat by the Corporation along with his Freedom for drawing the Plan of the intended Town Hall, as ℘ Receipt, No. 1	4.	14	6.–
29th.	Paid Expences at Serjt. Blands when treating about Gable End with John Thorley	–	2.	4½
Apr. 4th.	Paid Towers on getting down the Bell	–	–	6.–
	Paid James Bland's Bill for sundry Expences at different Meetings of the Committee as ℘ Bill – No. 2	–	19.	6½
May 3.	Paid a Man to Drink on driving Piles	–	–	1.–
5th.	Paid the Workman on laying the first Stone of the new Town Hall	1.	1.	0.–
7th.	Paid Expences at Serjt. Blands at a Meeting of the Council to Indemnify the Committee	–	7.	0.–
	Paid Expences at Serjeant Blands on laying the first Stone	–	5.	4.–
12th.	Paid Robert Dickinson for driving Piles &c ℘ Bill. No. 3	2	18.	8.–
14th.	Paid for Extra Hours, to save J. Whalley's Gable End	–	2.	0.–
June 2d.	Paid William Townson & Co. their Bill for Piles No. 5	8.	1.	0.–
	Paid Robert Dickinson for Sundry Extra Work No. 6	7.	3.	0½
7th.	Paid Sundry Expences at Overton to see the Quality of the Stone	–	9.	1.–
8th.	Paid Expences at Serjeant Bland's	–	1.	3½
15th.	Paid Expences on a Journey to Hornby &c. to meet Mr about the Stone for Columns	2.	9.	5.–
19th.	Paid Hugh Ravenscroft for the Use of two Sails to cover Mr Singleton's House End, as ℘ Receipt No. 7	–	10.	6.–
20th.	Paid Carting Furniture from the old Town Hall. No. 8	–	3.	0.–
27th.	Paid for Soft Soap for Piling Engine	–	–	1½
July 9th.	Paid Mr Stuarts Expences at Overton	–	3.	0.–
16.	Paid for Book &c for these Accounts	–	5.	0.–
Augt. 9th.	Paid Serjeant Blands Bill for Ale to the Workmen. No. 10	1.	6.	9½
	Paid Duke Holm for Eight Dozen of Piles No. 11	1.	12	0.–
12th.	Paid Mr John Brockbank for Slabs. No. 13	–	8.	8.–
	Paid for Nails	–	–	1
Sep. 5th & 17th.	Paid Expences to Damersgill with Workmen	–	7.	6.–
22d.	Paid Expences at Serjt. Blands	–	1.	6.–
–	Paid Workmen to Drink	–	1.	0.–
Oct. 2d.	Paid Expences at Serjeant Blands	–	2.	0.–
16th.	Paid Henry Walmsley for Advertizments &c. No. 16	–	7.	0.–
	Carried over . . . £			

A page from the accounts of Robert Tomlinson in the Bailiffs' Book for the building of the new Town Hall in 1781. It contains three references to the search for suitable stone at Overton (Bazil quarry), Hornby and Damasgill (Ellel).

The fells east of Lancaster also provided two other useful types of building stone. For the fire-places and parts of the flooring of the Custom House Richard Gillow specified 'Haw-Clough' or 'Clougha' flags.[11] Clougha, a prominent outlier of the Bowland fells, was the nearest source of fissile sandstone and different quarries produced different thicknesses and qualities.[12]

Thinner sandstone flags had been used for roofing since Roman times, and in the local vernacular of the 17th century a whole range of sizes were used; very large at the eaves and progressively smaller towards the ridge. By the

Gardyner's Chantry in St. Marygate. This group of four almshouses was originally founded in the 15th century and, unusually, survived the Reformation. In 1792 they were rebuilt at the same time as the large house immediately to the east, and detailed building accounts survive, rare for such modest structures.

mid-18th century, however, Lake District slate was becoming available. For the Custom House Richard Gillow specified;

> 'the Second Sort of Coney-Stone Slate equally as good, as that upon Captn. Henry Fell's new House at Fleet Bridge' [13]

The tradition of stone guttering, a feature of the 17th century, was coming to an end. On most Georgian buildings in Lancaster lead flashing and lead-lined guttering with downspouts cast or rolled out of lead were becoming commonplace. Lead of various weights per foot is carefully prescribed for various functions in contemporary building specifications, such as that for the Town Hall in 1781.[14] Presumably the growth in the use of lead reflects its greater availability by sea, via the port.

Because of the ready access to good stone Lancaster had no need for much brick building. Indeed a description of Lancaster in 1825[15] declared that the town had then only one such building. This was probably the Poorhouse in Wyresdale Road, a building of 1787–8, now gone. Brick was, however, used extensively where it was not seen. The arches under the portico of the Custom House, for instance, were turned in brick, presumably for greater ease and lower cost. The rear wing of nos. 1–3 Cable Street is also in brick, a very rare example of its external use in Lancaster, dating from 1759. Perhaps Richard Gillow, with his London training, had no personal prejudice against the use of brick but was prepared to acknowledge the local desire for facing in stone.

During the restoration of the Custom House in 1983–4 it was found that away from the front elevation many of the walls were effectively of timber box construction, infilled with brick and faced in stone rubble. The use of structural timber to tie and stiffen walls even in quite sophisticated Georgian buildings has been noted elsewhere.[16] In Lancaster it can be found in lintels over doors and windows and as bressumers buried within the stonework. Much old roofing timber was probably recycled in this way.

Useful building accounts survive for the Custom House, Town Hall and Assembly Room.[17] Among lesser buildings we have some useful accounts for the rebuilding of Gardyner's Chantry as four small cottages in 1792.[18] Unfortunately all too little is known about private houses. We do, however, know that experience from Capt. Fell's house, then recently built, was incorporated into the Custom House, so it is likely that much the same procedures and specifications were used. By today's standards these specifications were ridiculously brief and allowed of differing interpretation.

Of course many of the masons were working in a long tradition and needed only a front elevation or details of windows and doors to produce a respectable building. Argument sometimes sprang from the vagueness of the brief and could lead the architect and the builder into

1 and 3 Cable Street, photographed in the 1920s when the railings to the front were complete and before the lefthand half was unceremoniously beheaded. What makes this act of vandalism even more sad is that this pair of houses (of the late 1750s) is one of the very few that can be certainly attributed to Richard Gillow, architect and cabinetmaker.

Lancaster Castle in 1778, from a drawing by Thomas Hearne, on the eve of the rebuilding which was later to transform it. Virtually everything visible in this view is of medieval origin, apart from the rather weak curtain walls which replaced those demolished at the end of the Civil War.

conflict with the client; this occurred at both Glasson Dock and at St. George's Quay, where both clients and masons were unfamiliar with the work.

Architects

Many of Lancaster's Georgian buildings were not formally designed by architects at all but were, in the fashion of the time, put up by master masons working from pattern books. Practical solutions, born out of long experience, were found to problems which arose in construction. Even where there was an architect matters of constructional detail were often left for the mason to sort out. Usually the mason acted as foreman and clerk of works all in one.

Architects found themselves increasingly in demand, however, and particularly for public buildings. Lancaster was fortunate in having the services of two men, Richard Gillow and Thomas Harrison, who were architects of a very high standard. Other names of the period were Major Thomas Jarrett, Henry Sephton, and Joseph Gandy. The architect and builder of the Aqueduct Bridge, Alexander Stevens, is also worthy of mention. This was his last and finest work – he died in 1796 before it was completed – and possibly the finest piece of canal architecture in the country.[19] His monument can be seen on the south wall of the Priory church. Apparently his son, of the same name, carried on working as an architect in Lancaster for many years after and it is surprising that we can not identify a single building which he may have designed.

Richard Gillow, b.1734, was the son of Robert Gillow, founder of the well-known Lancaster cabinet-making firm. He was trained in London by William Jones, a minor architect. Gillow's training in architecture may have been aimed at to helping the firm move into lucrative interior design as well as furniture. At all events Richard did not have much time for his architectural practice because the cabinet-making business was doing so well. A number of buildings may be ascribed to Gillow, including the Custom House, a double house in Cable Street (nos. 1–3), and possibly also the Catholic chapel in Dalton Square (now Palatine Hall). (The Gillow family were Roman Catholics). The new Shambles was another important commission of the 1760s, but nothing survives of it. Undoubtedly there were several others.[20] The Assembly Room has been put forward as Gillow's work, and it is very probable that the musicians' gallery inside is a product of his firm.

Thomas Harrison came to Lancaster in 1783

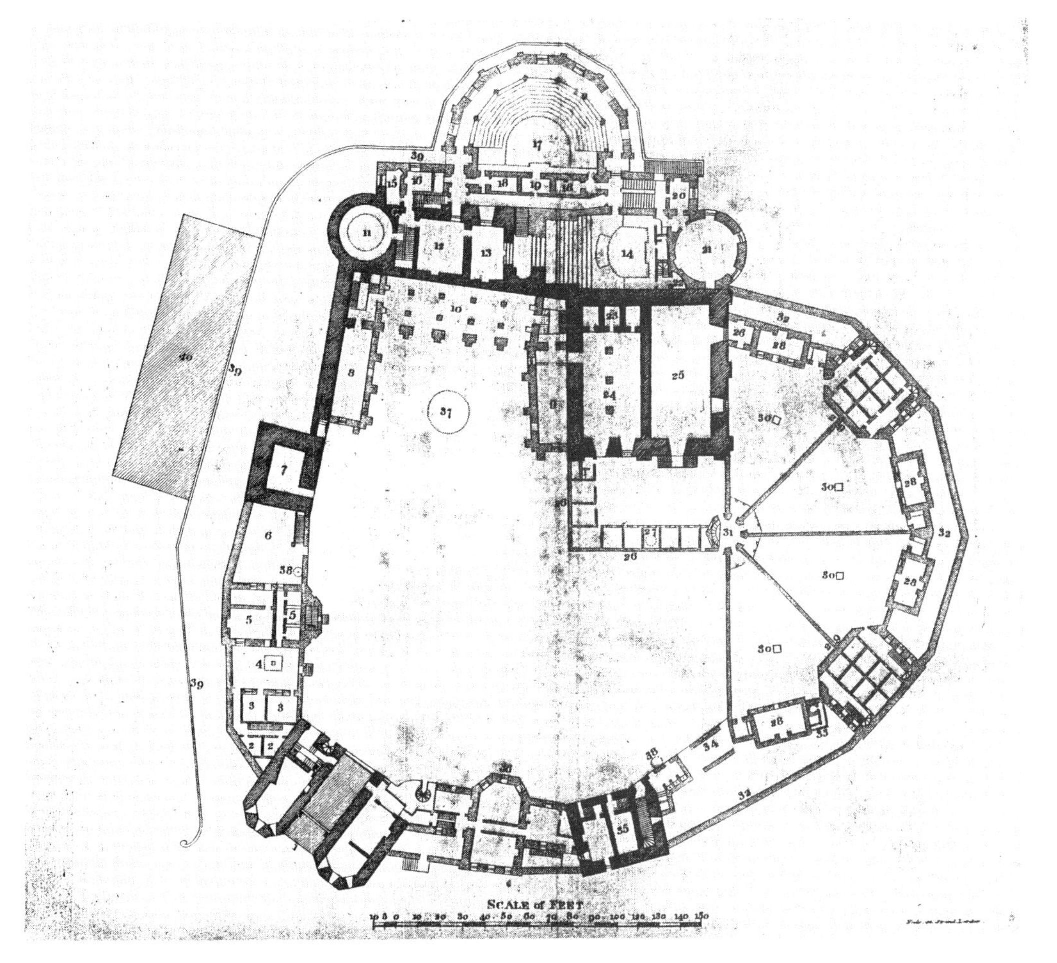

Plan of Lancaster Castle showing the alterations carried out up to 1807, from Clark's *History.* These include the Shire Hall and Crown Court, together with the new gaol buildings to the north. Later work included the Female Penitentiary to the south, replacing the old Dungeon Tower.

from Richmond, Yorkshire, after winning the competition to design Skerton Bridge. During the next ten years he made himself indispensable to the Corporation and was called in to draw up a number of plans and layouts. His Lancaster buildings include Skerton Bridge, the tower of St. John's church, added in 1784, the cupola of the Old Town Hall, an alteration of 1783 from Jarrett's original plan (q.v.), and Quernmore Park Hall, three miles to the north east.

His principal work was, however, upon Lancaster Castle where he started in 1788 upon the Shire Hall, and left, after many recriminations, in 1799, his work still incomplete. During this period and again up to c1823 the medieval castle was transformed into a modern prison with new courts etc.

Harrison was latterly working on both Lancaster and Chester castles, where he can be seen respectively in Gothick and Grecian mood. He did not live in Lancaster after 1793.[21] His work on Lancaster Castle was continued by Joseph Gandy.

Henry Sephton is known for only one building in Lancaster. Sephton, a Liverpool man, designed the new tower for the Priory church between 1753

Lithograph view of Lancaster Castle from the south-west by Jonathan Binns, *c.*1820, showing the new Shire Hall.

and 1755, after the collapse of its predecessor.[22] While it has one or two contemporary features it is otherwise very much in the revived 'Gothick' style, a very early example. It has a mixture of styles – a chinese chippendale fret on the transom, a chubby Georgian angel above the louvres, and Gothic crockets.

Major Thomas Jarrett, architect of the old Town Hall, was a retired Irish military engineer. He appears in the Army List as 'Engineer Captain in Ireland' since 1766 and Major since 1780, and must have come to England very shortly before, perhaps on resigning his commission.[23] The somewhat massive and old-fashioned building would suit very well an architect more accustomed to barracks and military works. Since the Genealogical Office in Dublin Castle was designed *c.*1760 by a Joseph Jarrett[24] there may well be a family connection.

Edward Batty is another architect of whom we know very little. There is no single building with which he can now be associated, but his name appears on a handbill in connection with the sale of land by the Dalton estates in 1783. He was subsequently responsible for the layout of Dalton Square and its associated streets in the same year, if not for the design of specific buildings.[25] Plots of land were sold off and individuals had their own houses built, but to a carefully specified standard of height and finish.

When traces of the Dominican Friary were found in the construction of Sulyard Street, it was Batty who measured and described the remains. He died 22nd February 1807 aged 67 and is buried at St. John's. His tombstone, which describes him as 'Architect', can be seen at the south-east corner of the church. Other sources, however, record Batty as a joiner and cabinet-maker living in Chapel Street in 1794–6,[26] so 'Architect' is perhaps a title to which he aspired.

Another shadowy figure is that of William Coulthart, who practised during the 1820s and 1830s in both Greek Revival and Gothic style. His work is known at Halton, at the Hall and the Rectory, and he carried out designs for a new vestry at the Priory church in 1827. Later he moved to Leamington Spa. A Trade Directory of 1834 records the address of his Lancaster office as Castle Grove.

More research needs to be carried out to establish his oeuvre.

Masons and Craftsmen

It has already been remarked that in many building projects the roles of mason and architect had not yet been fully separated.

Some of the early mason/architects have left no documentary trace, but we know of two from the late 1670s because they worked on the harbour at Whitehaven.[27] Richard Caton and Roger Lawson were Lancaster masons called in to solve problems in building the piers there. Perhaps they had gained experience from building quays on Green Ayre for various merchants. At all events Richard was drowned in 1680 and Roger left the works. While they date from before the period of our study it is clear that Lancaster had a rebuilding boom in the late 17th and early 18th centuries. Men such as these had expertise and were in considerable demand. We know from the autobiography of William Stout that in 1739:

> 'There being many new buildings erected in the town this year, the masons and wrights were so fully imployed that it prolonged the time in finishing it [sc. Stout's new house].'[28]

The successful tenderer for the Custom House in 1762 was the mason Richard Fisher. He, with Robert Clarkson, slater and plasterer, and William Sharp, plumber, was left to interpret the plan and the very brief details given by Richard Gillow, and to turn them into the building we see today. Some of this team had already worked together on St. George's Quay and on the Assembly Room a few years earlier. At the latter building Bryan Clarke, William Kirkby and Richard Fisher had been the masons. Fisher seems to have been the junior at that time but between 1759 and 1762 his stock had risen. He had obtained his freedom in 1753–4, while his older partners had been made freeman in 1739–40 and 1738–9 respectively. He seems to have died before 1796, when his heirs held four houses (built by him?) in St. Leonardgate and one in Penny Street.[29]

Robert Fox worked as carpenter on this job and on two other houses built for the trustees of William Penny in 1757. He died before he could be paid, but his widow eventually received the money owing. Other names occurring in the building accounts are Stephen Wildman, glazier, John Christopherson, plasterer, James Warriner, glazier and plumber and John Roper, smith (no doubt he supplied hinges, locks, nails etc.)

In the work on the two house mentioned earlier the carpenter was paid £58 and Robert Bennison and William Crook, masons, only just over £19. This suggests that these buildings were still essentially timber-framed. In such cases the carpenter would no doubt have acted as site foreman over the minor trades represented, while a mason would occupy this role in a mainly stone building.

The grouping of several masons to undertake work was probably a result of payment only being made after the whole job was finished. A single mason might well encounter problems of cash-flow, while several together could spread the burden and find guarantors for their debts, or for the bond they had to enter into, in order to guarantee completion of the work. The successful tenderers for the Town Hall in 1781, Robert Charnley, mason, and Robert Dickinson, carpenter, had to enter a bond of £3,000 before starting work.[30]

Charnley was working at nearby Glasson on the new pier in 1781 when he made the contract. There are very full building accounts for the old Town Hall among the Corporation Records.[31]

The contract to build the important and expensive new bridge, now known as Skerton Bridge, between 1782 and 1788, was signed by five masons of the Muschamp family, along with two others. Several of the Muschamps were from Otley, in Yorkshire.[32] Their joint venture may indicate a pooling of family resources to find the costs of materials and tide them over the period until repayment. It is not known whether the same masons built the Bridge Houses, the complex at the south end of the bridge which included the toll-house. Thomas Harrison was certainly the architect of both bridge and houses.

Christopher Clark tells us[33] that in the very considerable rebuilding works at the Castle up to 1807 the superintending mason was Alexander Hayes while the principal carpenter was Edward Exley. Neither man is recorded as working on other projects in the town, so in all probability they had been brought from elsewhere to oversee the work. Much further work is required to establish which other craftsmen were working on the Castle in the late 18th and early 19th centuries. It is clear that the project offered very substantial contracts and employed many men. Joseph Muschamp, one of the masons employed in building the New Bridge, appears as a supplier of stone to Thomas Harrison in 1791 'for the Works at Lancaster Castle'.

From the Corporation records it is clear that a number of the known masons were also leasing quarries on Lancaster Moor, so that they controlled the whole process from quarrying to setting stones. Lists of the lessees of the quarries survive for 1752 and 1756[34] and a plan of the quarries for 1814.[35]

A more detailed examination of Lancaster's Georgian masons appears in *The Local Historian*, for May 1991.[36]

Style and Design

From the beginning of the 18th century new ideas began to filter into Lancaster. The process took a long time; builders still used traditional methods and the vernacular style common in the 17th century continued in use in many smaller buildings. What began to be used more frequently, particularly for larger buildings, was Classical detail and Classical symmetry, derived from study of the ruins of Rome, the writings of the Roman architect and engineer Vitruvius, and the work of Italian architects of the Renaissance.[37]

To start with most influence came from the latter source, at second hand from the works of Palladio, Serlio and others. Gradually English architects became aware of other and older Classical ideas and some were able to see at first hand the ruins of Roman and Greek buildings, revising in the process their view of what was 'correct'. Thomas Harrison was one such, and his style reflects his understanding of how the various parts of a Classical structure fit together to form a harmonious whole. Many architects were very eclectic, taking separate details from different originals.

St. Nicholas Street Chapel, built by the Presbyterians in 1786 and demolished in 1967 to make way for a new shopping development. It is surprisingly sophisticated compared with many other Georgian nonconformist chapels.

Greece had been virtually inaccessible to early 18th century travellers, but in 1762 James ('Athenian') Stuart and Nicholas Revett published the first volume of *The Antiquities of Athens*, which for the first time made available to architects and dilettanti the unexpected wealth of Greek architecture. One of the buildings they illustrated was the little Choragic Monument of Lysicrates, built in 334 BC to commemorate victory in a choral competition, but in the 18th century forming part of the monastery of French Capuchins in Athens. This was Greek architecture on a conveniently small scale – the original monument is only nine feet in diameter – and it attracted many copies. Thomas Harrison used it twice in Lancaster, once as the basis of his design for the cupola on the old Town Hall and again for part of the tower of St. John's church. It was also to reappear many times in the guise of a temple in gardens of country houses.

Soon a number of books containing details of windows, doors, chimneypieces and even house plans began to appear. These were seized avidly by jobbing builders who could turn them into three dimensions. With them, however, came a growing understanding of proportion and it is this which often gives quite a simple Georgian building its air of distinction.[38]

At the centre of the problem of transferring Classical ideas to houses, churches and public buildings in 18th century towns was the fact that the prototypes were mostly temples, baths etc. Terraces of houses, for instance, required the devising of a new grammar for their design and ornament. Many public buildings had to be fitted into cramped or awkward sites, enforcing irregular ground plans. Churches traditionally needed towers, but there was no Classical precedent for these.

Many of the new ideas had, of course, been tried out first in London, Bath and other cities, or in the country houses of the rich.[39] The translation of Classical motifs to town buildings was, therefore, no new thing. Lancaster, like many other towns enjoying prosperity and having

Lancaster doorways. *Above clockwise*: 76 Church Street, 1 Great John Street, 108–10 St. Leonardgate, 112 St. Leonardgate.

Lancaster doorways. *Above clockwise*: 9 Dalton Square, 20–22 Queen Street, 20 Castle Park, 4 High Street.

Doorhead of the *Ring O'Bells*, King street, carved with Roman military trophies.

aspirations to distinction, was able to benefit from the experience gained elsewhere in transferring good proportions combined with economy to modest houses.

Classical symmetry (by which you could, in effect, split a building down the centre so that each side would form a mirror image) was difficult to achieve with town houses. There was often, for example, no room for a centrally-placed doorway, because the plot size did not allow an odd number of bays (usually three or five).

The solution was often to group two or more houses together in order to provide a central feature such as a portico, a large Diocletian window, or a projecting bay. Such solutions can be seen in Queen Square, Queen Street, Cable Street and St. Leonardgate. In other cases symmetry was just not possible. The Ring O'Bells in King Street (now a public house) has a finely detailed doorhead and surround, but is four bays wide, so the main doorway is placed asymmetrically.

Public buildings, such as the old Town Hall or the Custom House, were able to present a symmetrical tetrastyle (four-columned) portico to the front, but in each case existing buildings abutted to one side. Even the Bridge Houses, built on a new and open site, present only one main face. At the back, detailing and the quality of masonry are much inferior. Probably Thomas Harrison supplied only front elevation details,

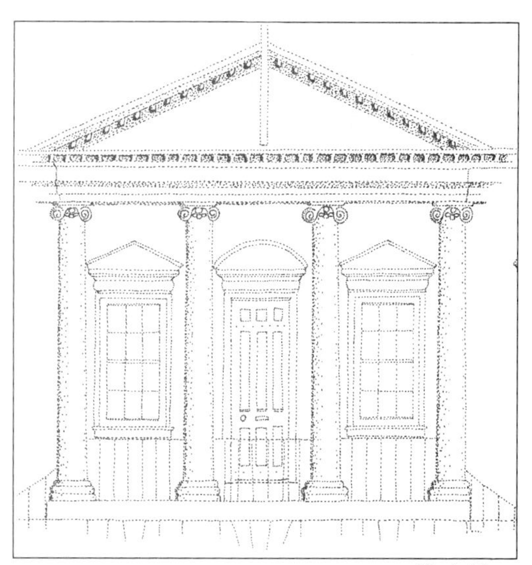

Wendy Moore

Ionic tetrastyle portico (on Custom House, St. George's Quay).

Rear elevation of shops in Sun Street, dating from the late 1790s, seen from China Street. The survival of the vernacular device known as the 'long stair window' is very striking.

which was standard practice at the time, and left the contractors to put the rest together.

Devices such as grouped doorways and porticos have already been considered. Windows were another important feature. The two commonest types used to provide a focus were the Venetian window, a tall round-headed central opening flanked by two shorter ones, and the Diocletian window, a half-round window suited to insertion in a pediment or a gable end and based on similar features in the Baths of Diocletian in Rome. From the northern vernacular tradition survived the very long staircase window, which can be seen best on the backs of houses in Sun Street.

Even ordinary plain windows vary a good deal, helping as they do to articulate and subdivide the frontage. Early in the 18th century very heavy plain monolithic surrounds were typical, but in buildings of good quality elaborate mouldings crept in by the 1730s and 1740s. These can be seen on the Conservative Club in Church Street or the house in Lawson's Yard just below the Market Square, now forming part of the Blue Anchor public house. By the latter end of the century those buildings employing large ashlars frequently have no stone moulding at all around the windows. The beauty of the stonework was allowed to show itself. Those walled in rubble were probably originally rendered or stuccoed. In such cases the mouldings served the function of marking the transition between surfaces.

Most Georgian windows have quite narrow glazing bars and the proportions created by the number and size of panes are very important in establishing the proportions of the facade. This is particularly noticeable where glazing bars have been removed and replaced by larger panes or double glazing. Sometimes the scheme of proportions is much more sophisticated, and involves the relationship between the width of the frontage and the height of the main floors, often the second and third storeys.

The size of a window, and the number of windows per room, was usually worked out by formula from the cubic capacity of the room. It is perhaps this relationship between size, function and proportion, together with a certain calm assurance, that gives Georgian buildings their essential fitness and charm.

Along with the changes in detail went changes of material. Roofs became less steep with the use of lead (on some public buildings) and slate, while the facades became taller in proportion to the whole building. The roof is often invisible from street level, being concealed behind a stone cornice. Lead gutters empty into lead or cast-iron downpipes, often with elaborate rainwater heads. Smaller windows at attic level, common in the previous century, disappeared and the new standard was the house of three or five bays width and three storeys height. The edges of the facade are frequently marked by quoins, large and slightly projecting blocks of stone, usually long and short alternately, which not only look good but also help to strengthen the corners.

In some of the larger houses such as 80, Church Street the kitchen and servants' hall are at basement level in the main block, while smaller servants' rooms seem to have been accommodated behind a balustrading at eaves level at 2 and 6 High Street. The loss of railings to many former basement areas has led to the blocking for security reasons of openings at this level. In Lancaster the usual arrangement was to provide the main front door access up a few steps, thus allowing the basement to be partly below pavement level and partly above. Consequently basement areas were not as dark and gloomy as they were in some Georgian towns.

At the rear of a number of properties of some standing, where they were accessible from a back street, were stables and coach-houses. Most of these have been converted to other purposes, such as garages, or sold off for business use. Several former coach-houses can still be seen in Bulk Street, behind Dalton Square, in Queen Street, and in Damside Street, where they served the houses on the north side of Church Street. No doubt the same buildings provided sleeping quarters for many of the men-servants. Maid-servants would probably have had garrets in the main house.

Services

One notable feature of Georgian buildings in Lancaster is the arrangement of a service wing projecting backwards, roughly half the width of the frontage. Here were often the kitchen and servants' rooms, and even additional family accommodation. In order to gain more light on the rear elevation of the main building the service wing often has a canted section at the point of junction. Where houses are in pairs the two service wings are usually built back to back with a common wall. Many of the plots available for building were long and narrow, especially those existing sites in the medieval core of the town. These long plots may have influenced the decision to build backwards rather than upwards.

Gardens and Summer-Houses

Little evidence survives for the layout of gardens. The central area of Lancaster was quite densely packed by the mid-18th century and here gardens were a luxury. Mackreth's map of 1778 shows quite convincing details of planting, and so does Binns' map of 1821, but it is impossible to be sure whether these layouts are real or merely conventional. An archaeological excavation of the garden of 4, The Circus, Bath – admittedly grander than any Lancaster house – suggests that a town garden would contain ornamental plants in circular beds and lines of small trees, but instead of lawns there would be rolled gravel walks.[40]

One or two gardens were more elaborate than

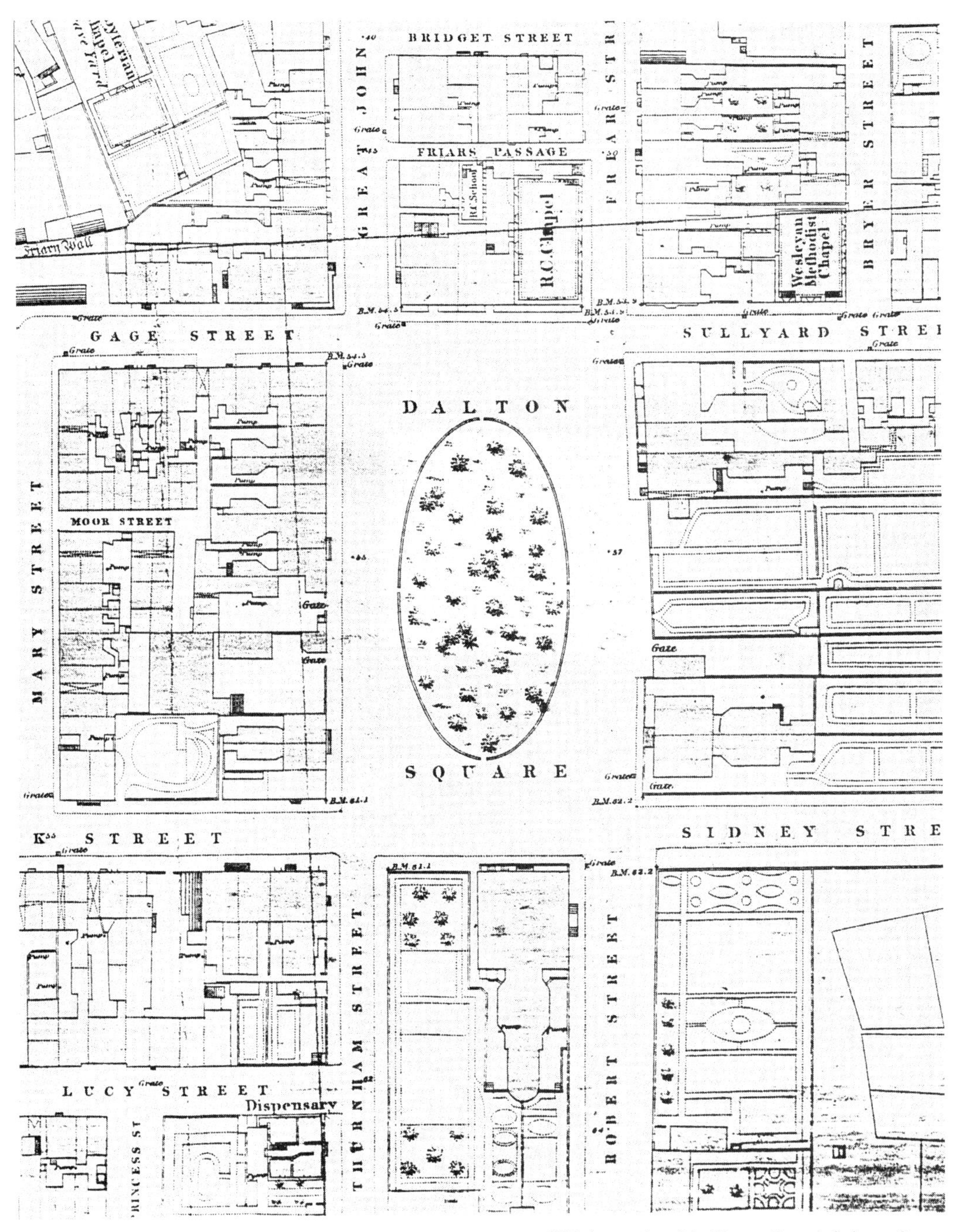

With the sanction of the Director General, Ordnance Survey

Detail from the 60" Ordnance Survey map of 1849 showing houses around Dalton Square. Many of them have a type of rear service wing which seems to be distinctive to Lancaster, with a narrowing of the wing and a canted section allowing light to the rear rooms of the main block and in particular to the long stair window at the junction. The canted or chamfered section is often of ashlar, compared with the coursed rubble of the service wing, because it could be seen from the main rooms.

usual. The house of the Sherburne family of Stonyhurst in St. Nicholas Street had a notable mulberry tree in its garden.[41] Behind the Sun Inn was a detached garden belonging to the Marton family whose house was 76 Church Street. It contained both a planted area and a bowling green, and its most notable feature was a very ornate summer house now known as the Music Room, although it seems only to have gained this name in the 19th century. This building appears to date from the 1730s and contains some fine plaster work of the type produced by Italian craftsmen which can also be seen at Towneley Hall and at Burrow Hall.[42]

Another summer house stands at the end of the long garden of Greycourt in Church Street. One stood here in about 1724 at the time of William Stukeley's visit[43] but the present octagonal structure probably belongs to the 1770s. Bearing in mind the number of summer houses which have been identified in Kendal as a result of detailed survey work it seems likely that many former summer houses remain to be found on the ground or from maps in Lancaster as well.[44]

Poorer Houses

It is legitimate to ask – where did the poorer people live in Georgian Lancaster? The answer is not straightforward because the evidence is scarce. From various sorts of evidence the answer seems to be that some people lived in those older houses which had not been replaced; in particular

An interior view of the Music Room, prior to restoration. The fine plasterwork is thought to be by Italian craftsmen, some of whom are known to have been working in Lancashire in the early 18th century at Burrow Hall and Towneley Hall.

in areas like Lower Church Street, Moor Lane and Stonewell, where houses with thatched roofs are depicted by the artist Gideon Yates as late as the early 19th century.[45] Others lived in cottages in yards and courts contrived behind houses on the main streets. The process of turning into slums was well under way by the 19th century but from dates on houses such as 1701 in Swan Court, 1713 in Little John Street, 1714 in Simpson's Yard or 1741 in Golden Ball Yard[46] it is clear that the infilling of former gardens was established surprisingly early. Finally poor people were scattered throughout the town and though there were fashionable areas there were few 'ghettoes' – in fact well-to-do and poor must frequently have lived side by side. This is evident from the Window Tax Returns of 1766,[47] which show a fairly random distribution of names marked 'P' for poor.

This octagonal summer house stands at the northern end of the garden of Greycourt, 102 Church Street, and enjoys an outlook over the Vicarage Fields, open glebe land since the Middle Ages.

Where did the money come from?

Lancaster began the 18th century with many small tradesmen and shopkeepers. By the end of the century many of these people or their successors were calling themselves 'merchants' and had much broader horizons. The merchandise which they dealt with was principally from the West Indies or the Baltic and many dealt in commodities. From the middle of the century, however, Lancaster was heavily involved in the infamous slave trade, collecting slaves from Africa and selling them in the West Indies. This subject is dealt with very well elsewhere,[48] but Charles Dickens well-known passage from the 'Lazy Tour of Two Idle Apprentices'[49] sums up the attitude of post-Abolition times to the trade and its monuments;

> 'Mr. Goodchild concedes Lancaster to be a pleasant place, a place dropped in the middle of a charming landscape, a place with a fine ancient fragment of a castle, a place of lovely walks, a place possessing staid old houses richly fitted with old Honduras mahogany, which has grown so dark with time that it seems to have got something of a retrospective mirror quality into itself, and to show the visitor, in the depth of its grain, through all its polish, the hue of the wretched slaves who groaned long ago under old Lancaster merchants. . .'

New Developments

While many of Lancaster's 18th century buildings occupied old sites in the principal streets a series of new developments occurred which took houses outside the previous built-up areas.

The first of these, carried out in a more or less haphazard fashion, was the development of the Green Ayre. The Green Ayre was a crescent-shaped area of land lying between the river Lune and the mill-stream, the latter's course marked today by the line of Damside Street.

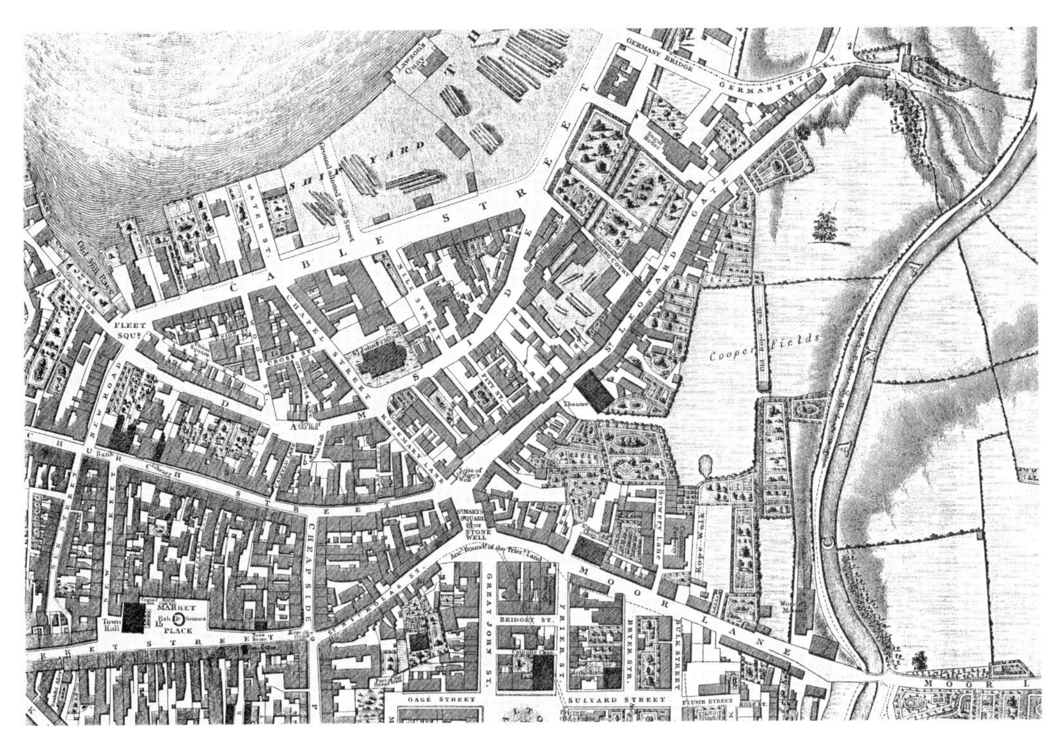

Part of Jonathan Binns' map of Lancaster of 1821, showing the north-eastern part of the town including the Green Ayre, the crescentic area to the top left of the map. This former island between the millstream and the river was one of the first to be developed, beginning in the late 17th century with a series of private quays. Cable Street was laid out with the view to becoming an impressive boulevarde giving access to the town from the new bridge further upstream.

Originally this had been an area of open space, where citizens took the air in an evening and young people disported themselves.[50] Spillage of buildings on to this space began with the establishment of a series of private quays and warehouses for merchants in the late 17th century; the process speeded up in the 1740s.[51] St. John's church, built in 1754, marks a late stage in this phase, for the church was put there to serve the new population. Further development took place on another part of the Green Ayre later in the century, as we shall see. Although the southern part of the area became a slum in the 19th century a number of good houses can still be seen, particularly in Chapel Street.

The next developments, and certainly the first to a coherent plan, were those of St. George's Quay (begun 1750), New Street (*c.*1745) and New Road (1752). It had been the intention to call New Street 'Charles Street', but this was reconsidered after the Jacobite rising of 1745 rendered the name politically unsuitable.[52] New Street and New Road were designed to link Market Street with Church Street and Damside Street and were cut through between the medieval burgage plots. New Street retains many of its 18th century buildings on its western side, of which several are converted warehouses. New Road shows little of its 18th century ancestry but an interesting relic found here in 1990 during road works was the old 'sough' or stone-lined drain running down the centre of the roadway, presumably much as it was put in, in 1752.

St. George's Quay developed after an Act of Parliament of 1749 enabled the new Port Commission to go ahead with building its legal quays and associated warehouses.[53] A strip of land bordering the river was obtained from the Vicar, whose glebe-land it was, and a retaining wall erected along the foreshore. Against this was

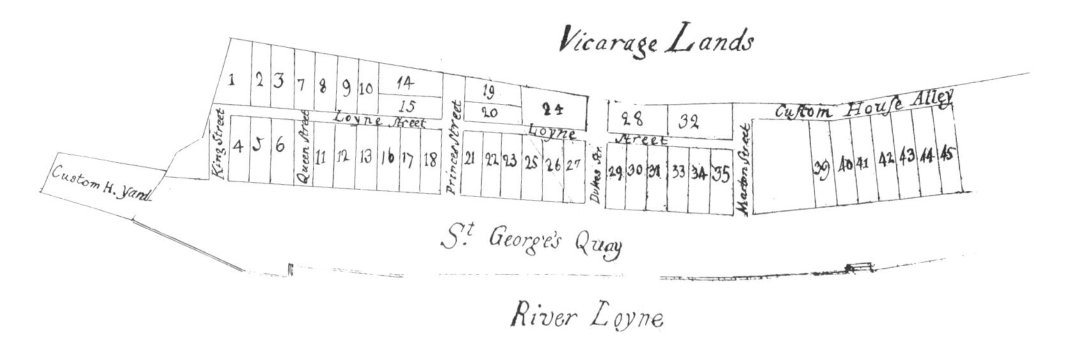

Building lots on St. George's Quay in 1754, reproduced from a sale plan among the Port Commission papers. Later on further building lots were let out to the west (the right on this plan). A triple size lot adjacent to lot 39 became the site of the Custom House in 1764, replacing the former Custom House further to the east. The whole development took place on former glebeland.

piled soil and stones, forming a level quay. In 1751, 1753, 1756, and again in 1781 building land was let out in lots.[54] Little control was exercised over what was built and a mixture of private houses, inns and warehouses, of varying character, resulted. Three lots were reserved for the building of a Custom House at the centre of the Quay. This was added in 1764, from earlier designs by Richard Gillow. St. George has never been particularly associated with Lancaster, so the naming of the quay is probably to be interpreted as a compliment to the reigning monarch, especially in the aftermath of the 1745 rebellion.

The Custom House, finished in 1765 and designed by Richard Gillow. Its front face is ashlar, its east side coursed rubble, its rear rendered, and its west face originally abutted other pre-existing buildings so was built 'overhand'. Such a prestige building saved most of its impact for the most visible face.

The warehouses are of a distinctive type of between three and five storeys. Large loading doors for each floor are flanked by windows. At the top a wooden or metal derrick provided the means of lifting goods from carts on the quay up to the main floors. There was no fireproofing, all the floors being of timber. Access from floor to floor was by a timber staircase in one front corner; most of these staircases have been removed in conversion. In between and behind many of the warehouses were merchants' counting-houses. Most of these have gone or been converted into houses.

After a long decline, caused by the failure of the trade for which it was built, this delightful riverside area is undergoing a renaissance, many of the warehouses being converted into flats.

Green Ayre saw a scheme for further development in 1784, when a plan was drawn up on behalf of the Corporation showing building lots for sale.[55] The new plan was associated with the building of Skerton Bridge, which was intended to provide a new and better approach to the town from the north. At the Lancaster end of

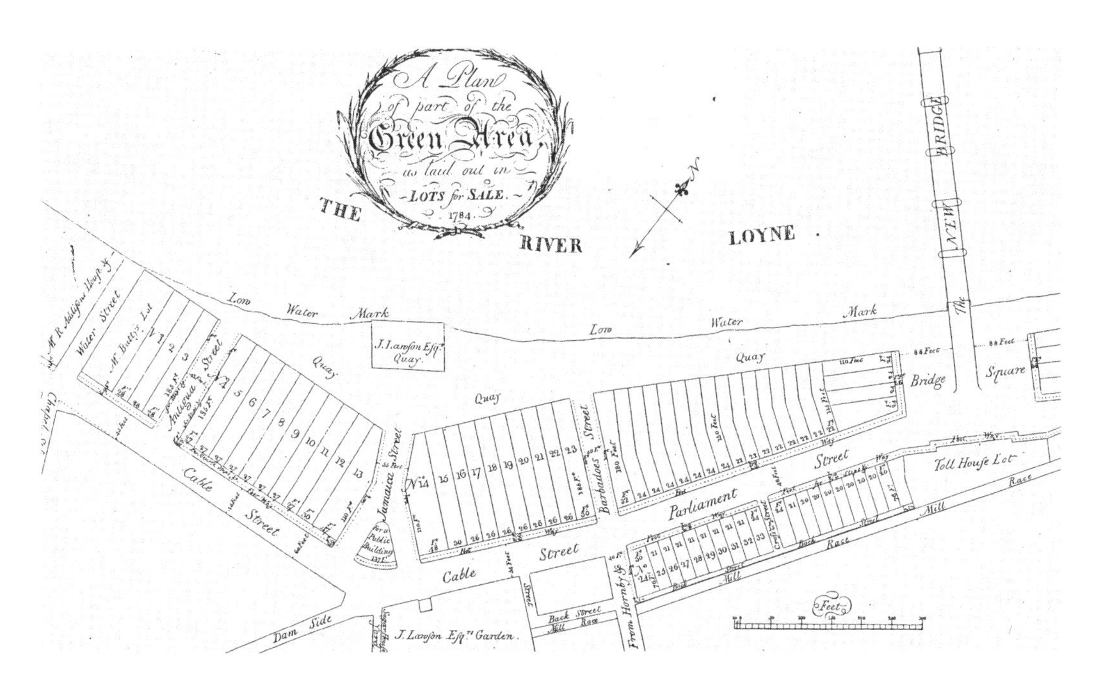

Plan of Green Ayre, marked out in building lots, 1784. Lancaster corporation was intending to capitalise on some of its spare land and at the same time to make an elegant approach to the town via Bridge Square, Parliament Street and Cable Street. The project never came off, the site later being taken for the Green Ayre station of the Little North Western Railway.

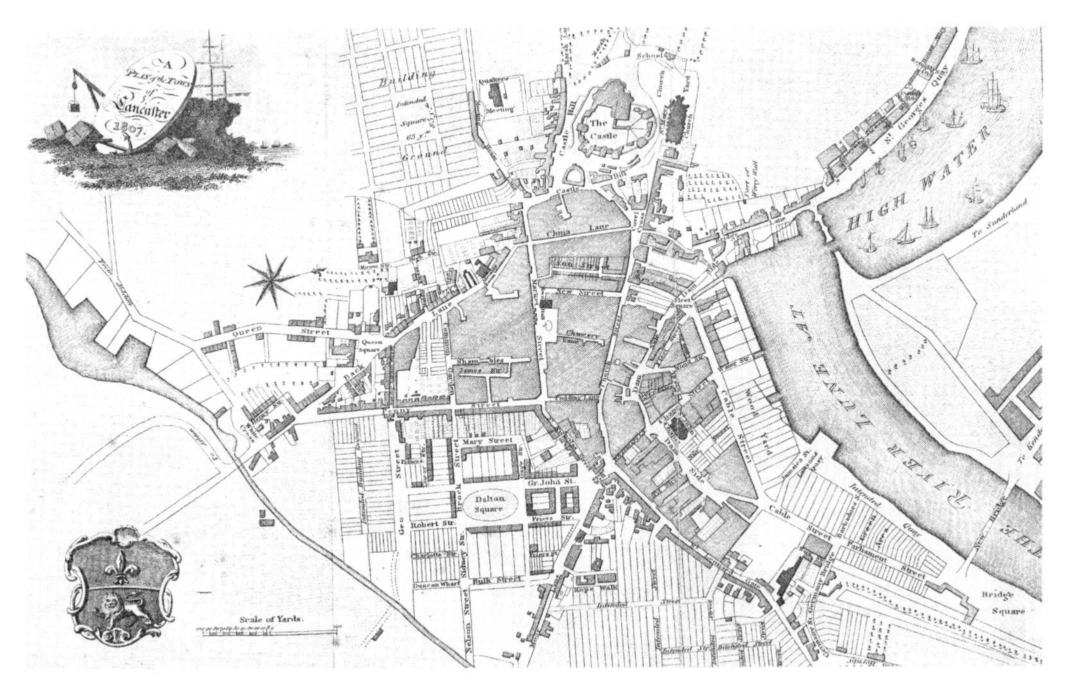

Map of Lancaster in 1807 from Clark's *History*. It shows very clearly the extent of intended development, especially to the east and west. Development eventually took place here, but not in the manner intended. Mid-Victorian working class housing of a higher density was to occupy much of the open area.

LANCASTER FRYERAGE.

TO BE SOLD,

On Friday *the* 3d *Day of* October, 1783, *at the Houſe of Mr.* Thomas Slater, *in the* Fryerage, *in Lancaſter*,

The Sale to begin at 7 o'Clock in the Evening,

On LEASES renewable for ever;

Subject to ſuch apportioned Ground Rent and other Terms and Conditions as will be produced at the Time & Place of Sale.

DIVERS LOTS OF

BUILDING GROUND,

In the FRYERAGE in LANCASTER,

Divided into a SQUARE and STREETS,

Agreeable to PLANS prepared;

AND WHICH

For Public Inſpection will be exhibited in the MERCHANTS' COFFEE-ROOM, the FRYERAGE HOUSE, at the OFFICE of *Mr. Barrow*, Attorney, and by *Mr. Edward Batty*, Architect, all in *Lancaſter* aforeſaid.

LANCASTER: Printed by H. WALMSLEY, Market-ſtreet.

Lancaster City Museum, LM 74.121

Left:
Handbill for the sale of building lots in the Fryerage, 1783. This was to be the site of Dalton Square. Edward Batty drew out the initial plan but the detailed design of houses was the responsibility of individual owners, within some general guidelines.

Below:
An engraving of 1807 after J. C. Ibbetson's 1798 painting of Lancaster from Cable Street. The smart new houses vie for attention with the town's rural and industrial aspects, marked by the cattle and the shipyard in the foreground.

the Bridge was to be Bridge Square, with a toll house forming one side. This, now known as the Bridge House, was the only building to be completed.[56]

Lining Parliament and Cable Street were to stand smart gentlemens' houses, not less than three storeys high. Other streets with names such as Barbadoes, Jamaica and Antigua Street, recalling Lancaster's trading connections with the West Indies, were to give access to the river bank. On the corner of Jamaica Street a triangular plot was reserved for a public building. Nothing of this was ever built. Clark's map of 1807 shows buildings only as far east as Water Street, an impression confirmed by J. C. Ibbetson's oil-painting of Cable Street in 1798.[57] It seems that an additional quay was intended to be built here, when the Old Bridge and associated hazards were removed.

The Corporation's aspirations were given a rude shock by a letter from Mr William Bradshaw of Halton, who owned fishery rights in the Lune and much else besides. He claimed that the proposed development breached his rights on the river bank, and threatened to sue. In turn the Corporation hastened to reassure potential buyers that it would defend their right to buy, in court if necessary. There can be little doubt that despite these assurances buyers were confused and put off. The threats effectively destroyed the development.[58]

In 1783 a handbill announced the sale of building lots in the Fryerage. This, the former site of the Dominican Friary, owned by the Catholic Dalton family who lived at Thurnham Hall, had obstructed the eastward development of Lancaster until now. John Dalton obtained a private Act of Parliament to break the entail on his estate.[59]

The new scheme, with plans drawn up by Edward Batty, was intended to create a large square with several elegant streets leading off. Building subsequently took place over a period of years, creating the present Dalton Square. Houses were individually designed and built, but had to conform to a standard of height, elevation, and finish;

Great John Street, looking north, prior to the building of the St.Nicholas Centre in 1967. These modest Georgian buildings, their ground floors taken over by shops, formed the northern fringe of the Dalton Square development. All were demolished in 1967.

'. . . each House shall be carried not less than three stories high above the Surface of the Ground . . .'[60]

The names of members of the Dalton family are enshrined in the street names – Great John Street, Mary Street, Bridget Street, and Gage Street, for instance. Access was gained to the new development from Penny Street by demolishing a house belonging to Mr. Brockholes; for short the new street was called Brock Street. Another access was via Ffrances Passage, named after the France family of Rawcliffe, who owned the land.

Most of the building lots in the new square were let out on forty-one year leases. The lessees were to build a pavement in front and might have cellar entrances not exceeding five feet in front, with railings or 'palisadoes'. Only houses, or a church, were to front the square, and nothing was to be built within the central oval without the approval of two-thirds of the owners.[61]

It appears that a number of the lots were acquired initially by speculators, and fairly quickly sold on. It was the second lessees of each lot who seem to have actually built the houses, or lived there. Lots 17 and 18, for instance, on the west side of the square, were let initially to John Brockbank and Luke Tyson. Christopher Bland, cooper, had acquired lot 18 by 1786 and lot 17 before 1793, when he had built houses on both

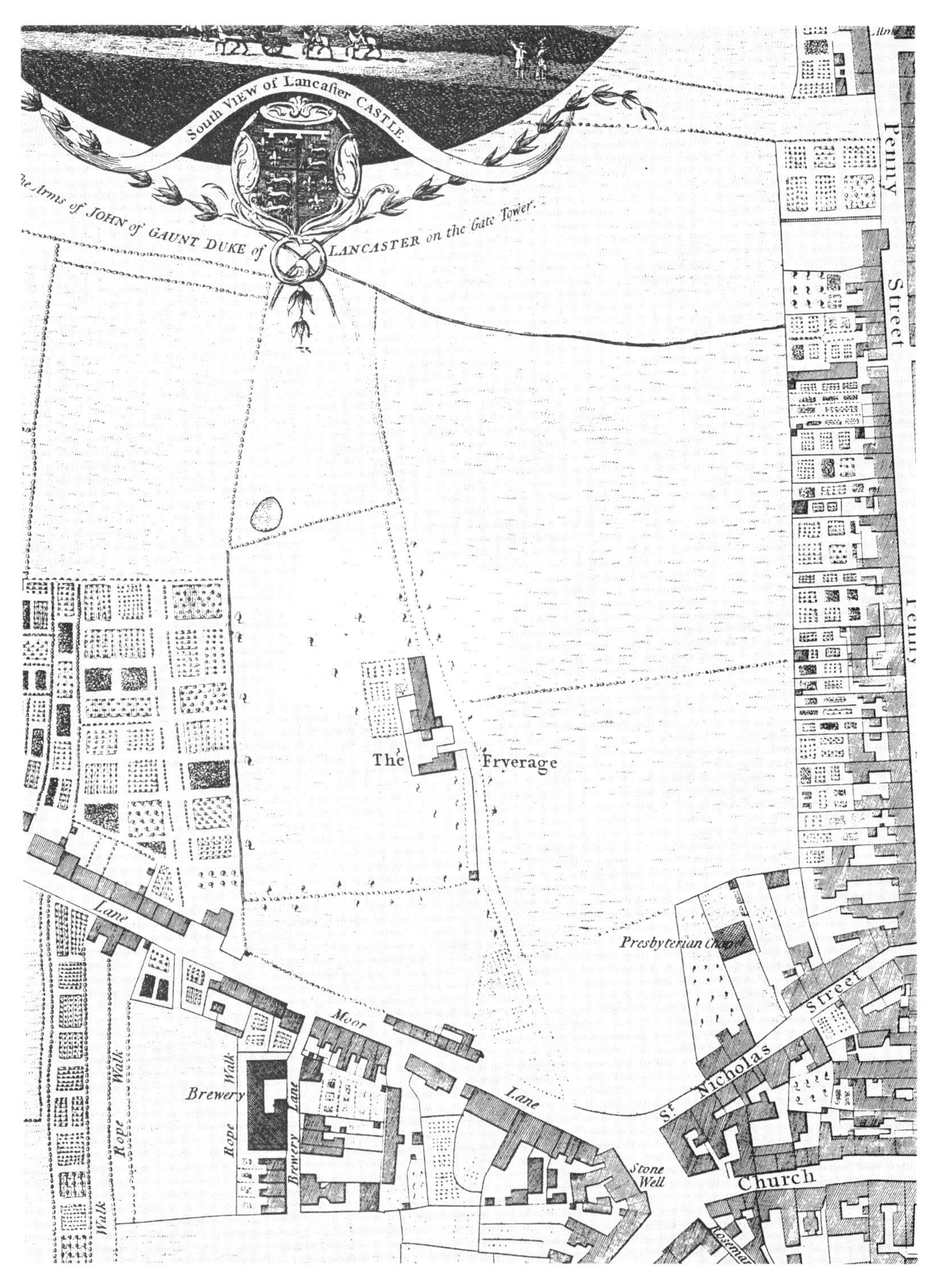

A section from Stephen Mackreth's map of 1778, showing the area of the Fryerage, a private house of John Dalton occupying the site of the Dominican Friary. This 10-acre polygon of ground, the former Friary precinct, was soon to be developed on behalf of the Daltons as a desirable residential area. Lots were initially let out on 41 year leases.

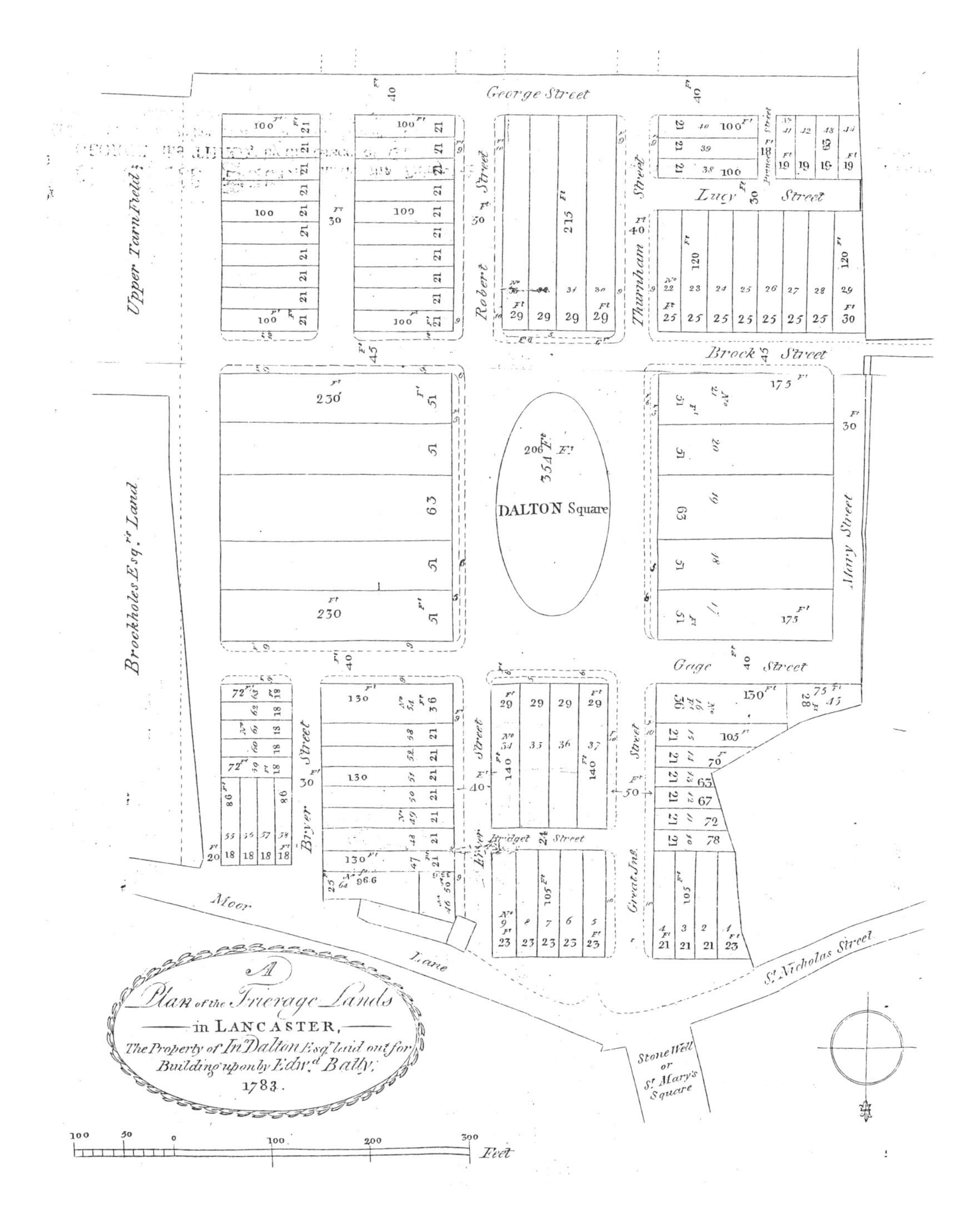

Plan of the Frierage Lands set out for buildings by Edward Batty, 1783. Dalton Square and the streets around it represent Lancaster's largest and most prestigious development in Georgian times, but many of the lots remain empty to this day, or are filled by inferior buildings. The whole project was conceived as a unity with large houses facing onto the Square from the east and west and smaller houses to north, south and at the corners; this is not how it was built. The destruction of St.Nicholas Street, Great JohnStreet and Gage Street in 1967 to build a new shopping development looks particularly insensitive when this plan is considered.

Dalton Square, looking north in about 1907. Work has already begun on clearing the 'Oval' or garden in the centre for the new monument to Queen Victoria, but the 18th century railings have not yet been replaced by stone balustrading. The absence of traffic gives the square more coherence than it currently enjoys. On the right is the original Roman Catholic chapel of 1798, by now superseded by St. Peter's Cathedral in East Road.

Nos. 10 and 11 Dalton Square, two of the grandest houses in Lancaster, were replaced by the new Town Hall in 1909. Built in 1791–4 by John Shaw and immediately sold on to Thomas Bond and John Hinde, these houses occupied four building plots and their gardens in Robert Street occupied several more.

and sold them to Robert Speight.[62] On the southern side lots 32 and 33 had been let by 1791 to John Shaw, who almost certainly built the pair of houses which formerly stood there, and he sold them in turn to Thomas Hinde and John Bond respectively.[63] The east side was the last to be developed.

Many of the houses were sub-let to tenants while a number of those on the western side of the square have lesser houses of broadly the same period built on the rear of their plots, such as those on Gage Street and Mary Street.

Despite the best intentions Dalton Square was never completed as planned, conceived as it was very late in Lancaster's age of prosperity. There are still a number of gaps, or inferior buildings, in Dalton Square and its environs.

Queen's Square (actually a triangle) attempted to give some grace to the southern approach to the town. In its original form it was much more

4 High Street, built in the 1770s for John Rawlinson, a successful solicitor. It later became St.Anne's Vicarage. The street in the foreground (Middle Street) is deliberately widened at the top to provide a vista of the house.

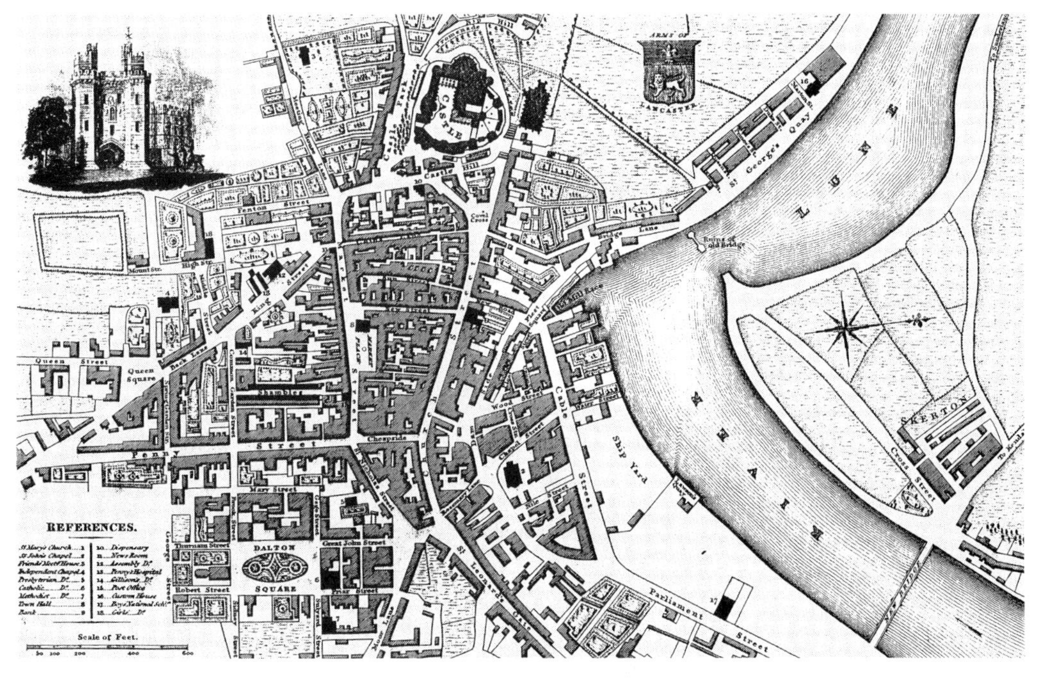

Baines' map of 1824 shows the town at the end of its Georgian development with the unfinished Dalton Square to the east.

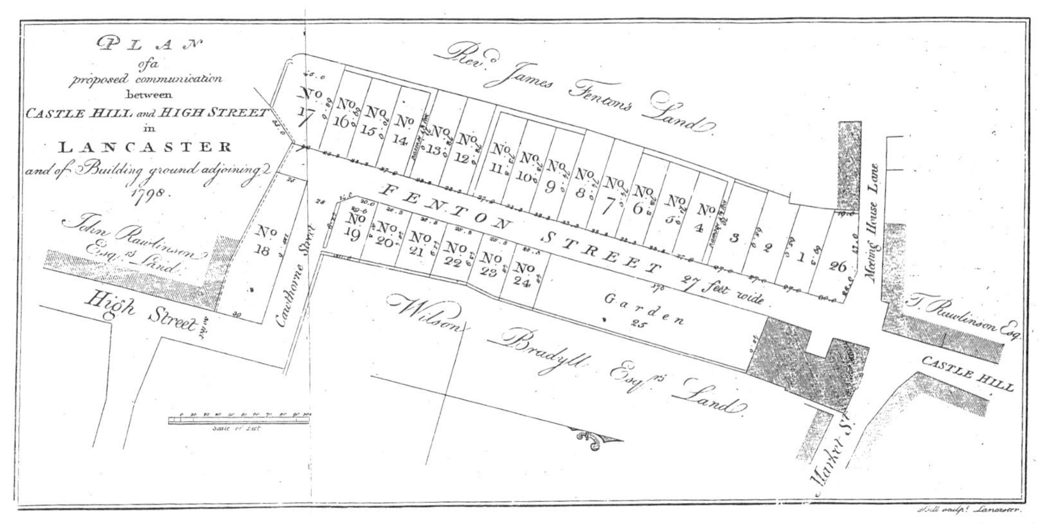

Proposal for a new street called 'Fenton Street', 1798. The site represents the gardens of Mr. John Fenton Cawthorne's house, on the Market Street frontage. No. 18 became the Girls' National School in 1820, and other buildings in the street date from that period.

enclosed than it is today; King Street was then a much narrower roadway and the great house of Mr. Bowes (now Falcon House) stuck out into it, only being cut back in the 1930s. Queen Street itself began to develop in the last quarter of the 18th century. It was not a planned development, but the houses were on virgin sites. Clark's map of 1807 shows further proposed building grounds and an intended square to the west of the town, bordered by High Street and Meeting House Lane. When building took place in this area it was much later, and to a different plan. An intended Wellington Street, to commemorate the hero of the Peninsula campaign, and running between and parallel to King Street and Queen Street, was put forward in 1813, but came to nothing.

High Street, then known as Mount Street, came into being as a result of the sale of Head Haugh field in 1770, by a Miss Gibson.[64] It was set out in eleven building lots and on these in due course were built High Street House, Garden Cottage and what was to become St. Ann's Vicarage. The owners of these properties were Thomas Saul and John Rawlinson. A number of plots clearly remained unlet and on one of these the Congregational Chapel was built a few years later.

Rather later came the attempt to develop the former gardens of the house owned by John Fenton Cawthorne, MP for Lancaster, at the top end of Market Street. A plan of 1798 shows twenty-six lots for sale on Fenton Street and Cawthorne Street[65] and in his diary for 16th September 1799[66] David Cragg wrote;

> 'Fenton Street just beginning building the first house . . .'

The house of John Fenton Cawthorne, MP for Lancaster, at the top of Market Street. It was demolished to make way for the Post Office.

The very plain and chaste doorway of the former Trades Hall in Fenton Street, typical of the restrained detailing of early 19th century buildings.

The Music Room, which now graces a square off Sun Street. Built originally in the 1730s as a summerhouse in pleasure grounds which then occupied the site of Sun Street it was already defunct by 1797. The building managed to survive, however, and was extensively and sensitively restored in 1974 by the Landmark Trust.

This development does not seem to have gone very well for in 1824 Fenton Cawthorne's house was auctioned along with twenty one building lots on both sides of Fenton Street.[67]

The house itself was bought for £1,550 by Leonard Redmayne, Director of Gillows, the cabinet-makers, but since again few of the lots sold another auction took place in 1827.[68] In 1820 one of the lots on the corner of Cawthorne Street and High Street had been given as a site for the Girls' National School. Many of the buildings in this street have been replaced by yards and sheds for the Post Office but the Trades Hall and a pair of adjacent houses probably belong to the late 1820s or 1830s.

Among developments within the historic core only one calls for attention. Former pleasure grounds lying between China Lane and New Street, containing the Music Room and a bowling green, were sold off from the Marton estates as building plots in 1797, producing what is now Sun Street.[69] The Music Room, bereft of purpose, languished neglected and in decay behind industrial outbuildings until its restoration to its original splendour in 1976 by the Landmark Trust.[70]

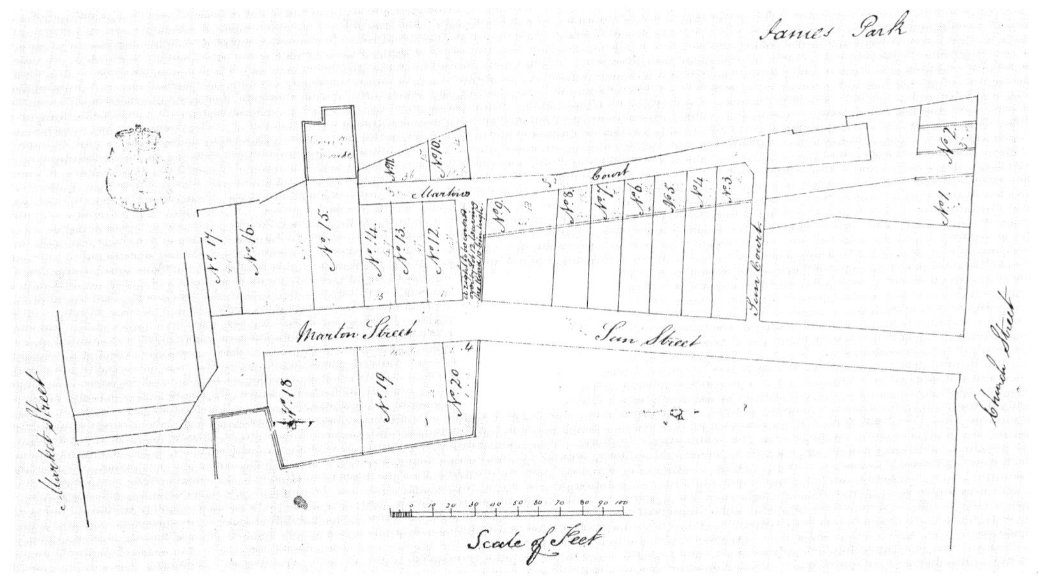

Lancaster Central Library, MS4479

Plan of proposed building lots in Sun Street in 1797, occupying the former pleasure grounds of Rev. Oliver Marton, who died in 1794. His son and heir was an imbecile, and presumably the Trustees of the estate were attempting to liquidate some of the Lancaster estates in order to provide him with a discreet living in the country. The 'Summer House', hemmed in by lot 15, is today known as the 'Music Room'.

Gazetteer of Georgian Buildings

CABLE STREET

Nos. 1 & 3

Remains of a pair of houses by Richard Gillow *c.*1759, with doors paired in centre. Six bays plus two extra bays at the side over a coach entrance x three storeys. Prominent keystones to windows, Doric columns to doorcases. Unusually for Lancaster the rear wing is of brick. The houses were built for Capt. Henry Fell and Mr Simpson.[71]

No. 5

House of five bays x three storeys. Centrally placed doorcase with Doric capitals.

Nos. 9 & 11

Two houses of three bays each x three storeys with a basement, the two doorways centrally placed under one pediment with Doric capitals and approached by steps.

Cable Street, looking west *c.*1925. The railings or 'palisadoes' of nos. 9 and 11, in the right foreground, are remarkably complete and show what has been lost elsewhere through road widening and wartime scrap drives.

Pen and wash drawing of the interior of Lancaster Castle in 1824 by James Weetman. On the left is the newly-built Female Penitentiary while the arcade in the centre surrounds the 12th-fcentury Keep. Weetman drew this from a window in the 'Pin Box', in the rear of the Gatehouse. As this was one of the Debtors' rooms, he may well have been a debtor himself.

Lancaster Castle

The great building programme between 1788 and 1823 included the Shire Hall, Crown Court, and Governor's house, designed by Thomas Harrison, and the Female Penitentiary and various other prison accommodation by Joseph Gandy.

The Shire Hall is a Gothick semi-polygonal structure with seven exterior faces, and a single Perpendicular window in each face. Behind it is the Crown Court, built against the outer face of the Lungess Tower, the medieval keep. The Governor's House was fitted into the site of the former curtain wall between the gatehouse and the Well Tower. Women prisoners were accommodated in a new range, the Female Penitentiary, one of the last major additions to the Castle, on the site of the medieval Dungeon Tower. The whole of the northern side of the Castle was also demolished and subsequently extended, with new towers for prison accommodation, before 1807.[72]

Lancaster Priory Church

West tower with pinnacles and pointed bell openings, designed by Henry Sephton of Liverpool *c.*1753–5, to replace a predecessor which showed signs of collapse after a misguided attempt by the Churchwardens to raise it in height by 'ten yards'.[73] A very early example of 'Gothick' style.

Castle Hill

Nos. 15–17
A pair of cottages formed about 1820 from a single house of 1739, with a datestone and the initials of the first owners over the door. It must have been typical of many of the more modest 18th century houses in Lancaster and is a rare survival, still entirely in the vernacular tradition of the previous century. Window mullions have been removed at some stage and one larger window provided on the ground floor to create a shop. Since 1978 the left hand half has been open to the public as a museum.

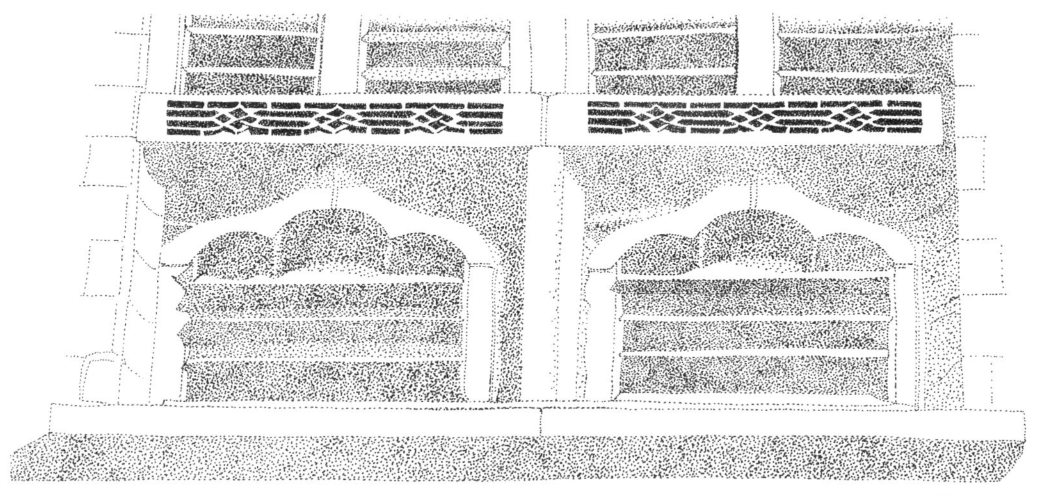

Wendy Moore

Above:
'Chinese chippendale' fret (on bell openings at Priory Church.)
Left:
The Dispensary, 19 Castle Hill, built in 1785 to provide rudimentary medical help for the poor. It is entirely domestic in scale and appearance.
Below:
Plan and sketch of 15–17 Castle Hill. Built in 1739 in the vernacular style of the previous century, with mullioned windows, it served as a house and a shop. In about 1825–30 it was divided into two, with a passage down the middle. Sash windows were inserted at this time. Gardens, a well, privies and outbuildings lay to the rear. The whole represents the survival of a once common type of artisan house in Lancaster, not very different from its rural counterparts.

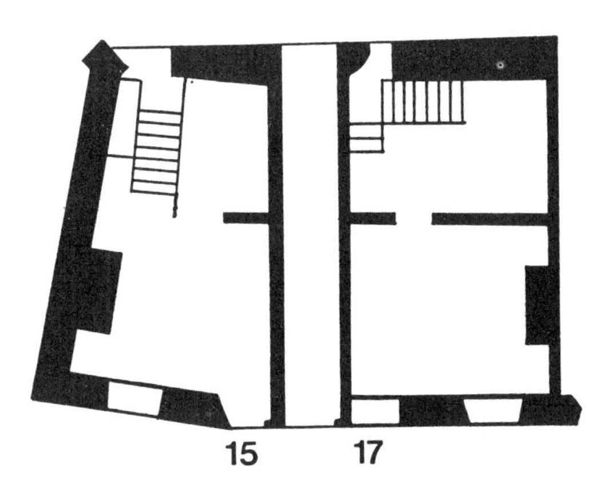

These Georgian houses with deep hood moulds over the doorways stood in St.Mary's Parade, opposite the Vicarage, until some forty years ago. They gradually decayed, became derelict, and were demolished. They formed part of an extensive group of post-medieval houses which gradually encroached on the old Castle ditch as it ceased to have any military function.

No. 19
Three bays x two storeys. Plain porch in front with a fanlight and Doric capitals. Cartouche above now reads 1845 but formerly carried the 'Good Samaritan' relief now at the Royal Lancaster Infirmary. A small but well-proportioned building dating from 1785 and built as a Dispensary, providing the first, and very modest, free health care for the poor. The original acroteria can be seen on the top and sides of the pediment.

CASTLE PARK

No. 2
Former George Fox School. Five bays x three storeys, very plain. Centrally disposed doorway. A semi-octagonal projection to the rear carries the main staircase, which may be a later addition.

Nos. 10, 12, 14, 16
A terrace of houses, the divisions unclear from the exterior. At the right hand end a carriage entrance. Two storeys, apart from no.16, which has been raised. Probably *c.*1730–40, since the land was acquired on a two hundred year lease in 1727. Dormer windows in the roof, probably not original.

No. 20
A very fine and dignified house of five bays x three storeys with a centrally placed doorcase, possibly later, with Ionic capitals. Datestone over the centre of 1720. Built originally for the Birdsworth family and later owned by the Satterthwaites, who were merchants. No. 22 was an addition while nos. 18 and 18a next door formed part of the stable and coach-house complex, now converted to separate houses. Attached is a privy house, containing a four-seater privy, three for adults and one for children!

No. 24
Five bays x three storeys. Elaborate quoins at the corners, very plain detailing. Later this house was occupied by the famous 19th century firm of Paley & Austin, architects. To the left is a later extension used by them as a drawing office.

Storey Institute
The rear gateway is composed of parts of the Tuscan porch and pediment of the house of Mr. John Fenton Cawthorne, MP for Lancaster. The house was demolished in 1921 and the site is now occupied by the Post Office building, opposite the Storey Institute.

CHAPEL STREET

St. John's Church
Simple Classical church of *c.*1755 with a nave of five bays and an apsidal east end. The gallery runs around three sides and the roof is carried on Ionic columns. The architect is unknown. Tower added 1784 by 'the ingenious Mr. Harrison'.[74] The upper stages of this tower are based on the

20 Castle Park is an elegant building of 1720 which was probably considered a novelty at the time, being one of the first symmetrical sash-windowed houses in the town. The datestone between the upper windows is the only vernacular feature visible on the front. The former stable and coach-house block to the right has been converted into other houses.

St. John's Church, Chapel Street. The nave is of the 1750s and the tower of some thirty years later, designed by Thomas Harrison. The upper stage of the tower, below the spire, is based on the Choragic Monument in Athens, a popular architectural form after drawings of the original were published in 1762. The church is in the care of the Redundant Churches Fund.

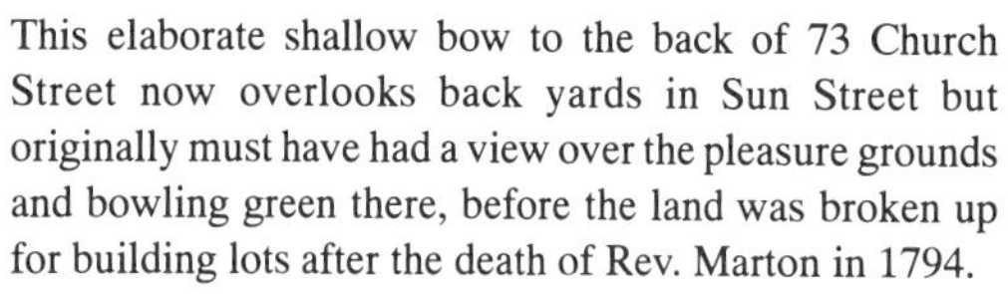

This elaborate shallow bow to the back of 73 Church Street now overlooks back yards in Sun Street but originally must have had a view over the pleasure grounds and bowling green there, before the land was broken up for building lots after the death of Rev. Marton in 1794.

This link extinguisher is a rare survival of the days before street lighting when links or flambeaux were carried before the coaches of latenight revellers. This one is on the wall of 76 Church Street. Others are to be seen in London and Bath.

Choragic Monument of Lysicrates at Athens.[75] Porch added in early 20th century. The iron gates date from 1818. Inside is a fine set of box pews.

CHURCH STREET

No. 65

Three bays x three storeys, the doorway placed asymmetrically on the left hand side with a small pediment and fanlight.

No. 67

Very similar, but with a plainer doorway.

Nos. 69 & 71

A pair of houses of three bays each x three storeys, the two doors placed together in the centre with a single plain pediment over the top.

No. 73

Four bays x three storeys, with the doorway placed asymmetrically at the right hand side. Rendered, with moulded window surrounds. Probably dating from the early 18th century. At the back is an odd bow running through two storeys and overlooking the rear yard. It makes more sense if we visualise it originally looking out over the pleasure ground and bowling green associated with the Music Room.

No. 76 (the Conservative Club)

This house, owned by the Marton family in the 18th century, has a composition of five bays x three storeys. Iron railings survive to the front on

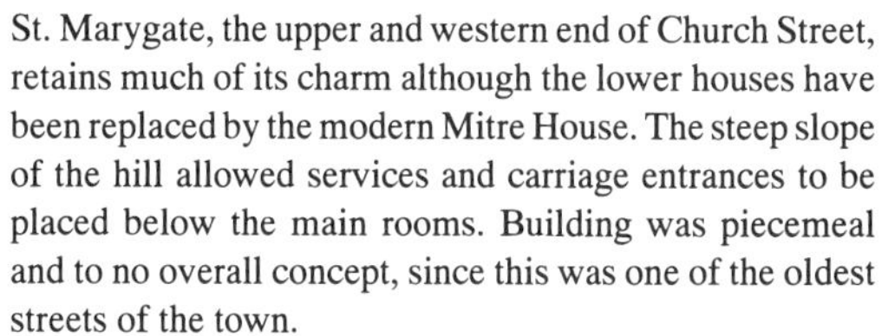

St. Marygate, the upper and western end of Church Street, retains much of its charm although the lower houses have been replaced by the modern Mitre House. The steep slope of the hill allowed services and carriage entrances to be placed below the main rooms. Building was piecemeal and to no overall concept, since this was one of the oldest streets of the town.

Window detail from Greycourt, 102 Church Street, built in 1792 for Mr. George Postlethwaite, illustrating the superb quality of the masonry. Unlike this example many ashlar faced Lancaster buildings have no architraves to the windows, allowing the ashlars to frame the window opening.

one side only. The doorcase has Ionic columns. Lead downpipes and rainwater heads with lion masks on them.

Behind the railings is a very rare link-extinguisher of the type seen in Bath. Inside the house there is some notable oak panelling with pilasters. The rear of the house is part of a much older building.

No. 78–80

Three bays x five storeys, the centre bay being a shallow elliptical projection; the doorcase has a Doric pediment. The building is known to date from 1772–5 and was built for Dr. Daniel Wilson, one of the Wilson family of Dallam Tower.[76] It has important plaster ceilings.

No. 96

House of four bays x four storeys, asymmetric, with no door at the front but instead a large carriage entrance, giving access to the side. The design is due to its sloping site.

No. 100

Three bays x three storeys plus a basement, asymmetric, with an extra window on the ground floor. The door set slightly to one side of centre. The design is again due to its sloping site.

No. 102 (Greycourt)

House of three bays x three storeys, with an entrance on two levels. At the first floor level, doorway leading in from the steep descent of St.

Mary Gate. At basement level an extra storey had been contrived out of the slope of the hill, giving a carriage entrance on the right hand side. This building is known to date from 1792, and was built for a Mr. George Postlethwaite.[77] At the far end of the garden an octagonal summer house, with one room per floor. There was a summer-house here in 1724 when William Stukeley came to Lancaster, but this one looks half a century later.

Next door to Greycourt is the site of Gardyner's chantry, a medieval almshouse. It was rebuilt in 1792 as a row of four modest cottages in the form of two pairs at the same time as Greycourt but was demolished in the 20th century. The 1792 rebuilding inscription survives built into a wall in the garden immediately to the west.

DALTON SQUARE

Where the Town Hall now stands were two very large houses, nos. 10 and 11 Dalton Square, built between 1791 and 1794, with large gardens to match. The west side of the square seems almost detached by the busy Thurnham Street and the buildings on this side have lost their original ground floor elevations to modern shop windows.

Nos. 1 & 2

All within one frontage and the same block as Palatine Hall. No. 1 runs round the corner and becomes No. 13 Great John Street. No. 2 is of three bays x three storeys with a centrally placed door on the ground floor. It was originally the Presbytery for the chapel next door.

Palatine Hall

Former Roman Catholic chapel of 1798. The Dalton Square frontage is of three storeys and three bays, just like a house, with a later, centrally-placed, porch. The side elevation, however, has a Venetian window and three tall round-headed windows. An Act of 1791 laid down the form of church Catholics were allowed to build and worship still had to be discreet.

No. 3 (Borough Club)

Three bays x three storeys with a centrally placed door on the ground floor and a porch carried forward on plain Doric columns. Built in 1824 on the site of the Frierage Coffee House.[78] Porch and windows altered later in 19th cent.

No. 4

A smaller and simpler version of No.5, and somewhat later. Two bays x three storeys. Simple doorcase with plain hood on brackets. Built after 1824, on the evidence that it was fitted into the space between No.5 and the Borough Club (qv), and is not shown on Baines' map of 1824.

No. 5

House of three bays x three storeys. The entrance has been placed asymmetrically to the left, approached by steps. Doorcase carried on Ionic capitals. Built between 1801–1810 for Jacob Ridley, merchant.[79]

Nos. 8 & 9

Pair of houses of three bays each x three storeys, the two doorways set together in the centre. Plain doorcases with half-round doorheads and fanlights. At the rear of each building is a typically offset service wing, this time containing a very long staircase window, and former coach-houses face onto Bulk Street.

FENTON STREET

Nos. 4 & 6

A pair of houses of two bays each x three storeys with simple porches on brackets. In the gable end of each a tall round-headed window. Built in the late 1820s or early 1830s.

Trades Hall

A substantial five bay x three storey building, the centre bay emphasised. Complex roof with dome over stairwell, which contains a 'geometrical' staircase, cantilevered out from the wall. Late 1820s or early 1830s.

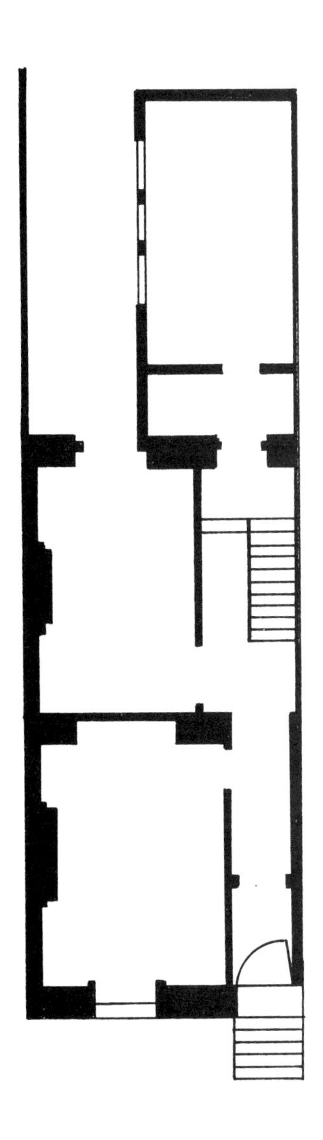

Plan of 4 Dalton Square, from a survey by S.Gardner (omitting later accretions). The house was built after 1821 between two existing buildings, whose outer walls it shares. Like its next-door neighbour it had a screen dividing the main ground floor rooms which could be opened up for entertaining.

4 Dalton Square. Despite its small size it copies many of the features of its neighbours (see plan).

5 Dalton Square, built between 1801 and 1810. For many years it served as the offices of the Lancaster Rural District Council and now it contains the City Council's Housing Service (see plan).

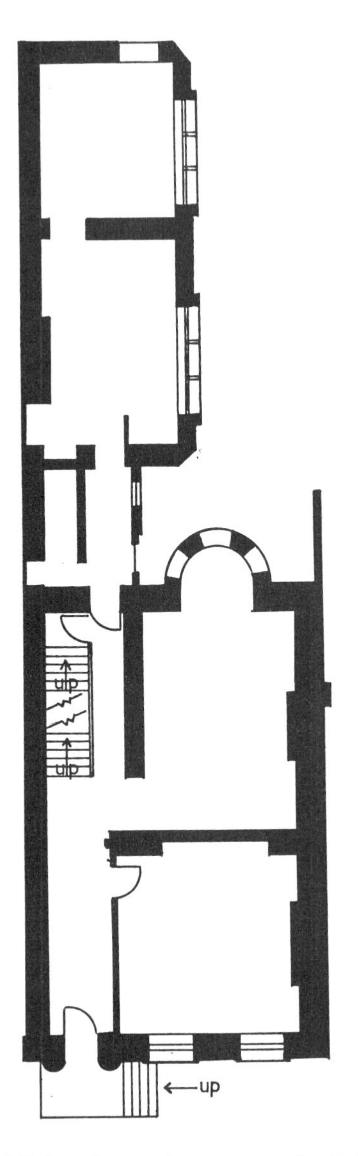

Plan of 5 Dalton Square, from a survey by S. Gardner (omitting later accretions). A screen divided the main rooms on the ground floor, presumably so that more space could on occasions be made available for entertainment. Services were provided in a rear wing, the inner corner of which was chamfered to allow more light to enter the elaborate bow window of the main reception room (reconstructed here from earlier plans and surviving masonry in the basement).

GREAT JOHN STREET

No. 1 (Formerly the Reform Club)
House of three bays x three storeys. Elaborate centrally placed doorway approached by steps. Venetian windows to ground floor. At third floor level in the gable there are lunettes. The miscellany of window types is a good example of 'pattern-book' architecture. This is part of the Dalton Square development and hence post–1784.

HIGH STREET

National School for Girls
A plain building of three bays to the front x eight bays to the side. An inscription over the front reads 'Built by public subscription AD. 1820 to establish Order, check Vice and uphold Virtue.' The lower part of the facade has been altered to make a shop front. The ground on which it stands was once part of Mr. Fenton Cawthorne's garden, which he gave to create the school.

Nos. 2, 4, & 6 (Former St. Anne's Vicarage)
Three houses forming one composition. The centre house of five bays x two storeys with a Diocletian window in the pediment and a Doric doorcase with a fanlight. Flanked on either side by two smaller buildings, one a house of three bays with a carriage entrance, the other a house of four bays also with a carriage entrance and the blocked remains of what seems to be a warehouse hoist slot. The two outer houses have balustraded parapets. This is one of the grandest houses in Lancaster, built *c.*1770 for Mr John Rawlinson, solicitor, but later used as St. Anne's Vicarage. The effect of looking up Middle Street to the principal house of this group was greatly enhanced by a subtle widening of the roadway to the same width as its facade.

Trinity United Reformed Church
Five bays x two storeys to the High Street frontage, with a door placed centrally. The windows with round heads and prominent keystones. The church dates from 1773 and was initially an Independent Chapel.

High Street House
Five bays x two storeys, extremely plain, the door approached by steps with a simple porch on brackets. Built for Thomas Saul in 1774.[80] Above the roofline there are projecting dormers, probably not original.

Opposite this is Garden Cottage, a small cottage ornee in the Gothick taste with pointed

Wendy Moore

Diocletian window (on no. 4 High Street.)

window and door-heads. On the High Street front it has three bays with a central door, now blocked, and in the side elevation a tall staircase window. A battlemented parapet completes the Gothick detailing. This property originally belonged to High Street House.

King Street

Assembly Room

An austere building of five bays x two storeys, put up in 1759 by the Trustees of Penny's Hospital (qv) as a means of raising income. The windows of the ground floor have quoins, those on the upper floor are plain. Small half round portico on four columns at the front. Instead of a lower right hand window there is a door, allowing separate access to the upper floor, so that two events could be held on separate floors without clashing. In the upper room is a wooden gallery with a chinese chippendale fret to the front, perhaps by Gillow.

The gallery in the Assembly Room in King Street. It is in the popular 'chinese chippendale' taste and was probably made by Gillows, *c.*1759, as part of the original furnishing

Penny's Hospital

A group of twelve small almshouses with a chapel, grouped round a quadrangle with an

Penny's Hospital, King Street. Now modernised inside but still used for their original purpose these almshouses were built in 1720 by Penny's Trustees in an old-fashioned style harking back to the previous century.

entrance gateway. A Latin inscription over the gate records a date of 1720, but the whole hospital seems much earlier in concept and design. The group of elderly Trustees of William Penny clearly favoured the architectural style of their youth.[81]

Ring o' Bells
Four bays x three storeys, a house of *c*.1720 with an elaborate doorcase, its head carved with military trophies. Doorway placed asymmetrically in the facade.

No. 93
House of three bays x three storeys. A fourth storey with dormer windows. Doorway set asymmetrically on right hand side with plain round-headed doorcase.

Market Square

Old Town Hall
Since 1923 the home of the City Museum this rather austere building is of five bays x two storeys, with a giant Tuscan tetrastyle (four-columned) portico carrying a pediment and a cupola. The cupola by Thomas Harrison, again based on the Choragic monument of Lysicrates, the rest of the building by Major Thomas Jarrett, 1781–3. Round-headed windows to both floors; the ground floor window-openings were originally doors to the corn-market and were closed at night by iron gates. The building was altered internally in 1874 and again in 1881 but has two original Gillow fireplaces on the first floor, moved when the rooms here were reorganised. Large garlanded urns originally crowned the pediment and outer corners of the building but were removed as unsafe in the 1950s.

Market Street

Lawson's Yard
Very battered remain of an elaborate six bay house divided into tenements and now incorporated into the Blue Anchor pub. Despite appearances to the contrary the windows have never looked out on any prospect other than the rear of the Blue Anchor.

At the top end of Market Street and in China Street there are several nice, small, Georgian buildings mostly with their ground floors spoilt by later and unsympathetic shopfronts.

The Friends' Meeting House in Meeting House Lane. Rebuilt in 1708 and extended in 1744 its growth mirrors the growing wealth and influence of the Quakers from radical outcasts in the 17th century to important members of the merchant community in the 18th century. For all that it retains the pleasing plainness which is a feature of so many meeting houses.

Meeting House Lane

Friends' Meeting House
A characteristically plain building of 1708, with an extension of 1744. The latter has a fine Venetian window, perhaps indicative of the change in wealth and attitude experienced by Lancaster Friends between these dates. Deep semi-octagonal porch to front. The internal fittings such as benches and stand for the elders do not survive, which is a pity.

Moor Lane

Duke's Playhouse
Former St. Anne's Church of 1796. On Moor Lane the facade consists of six bays and five windows with lunettes placed above them to light the former gallery. Doorway to extreme left. The

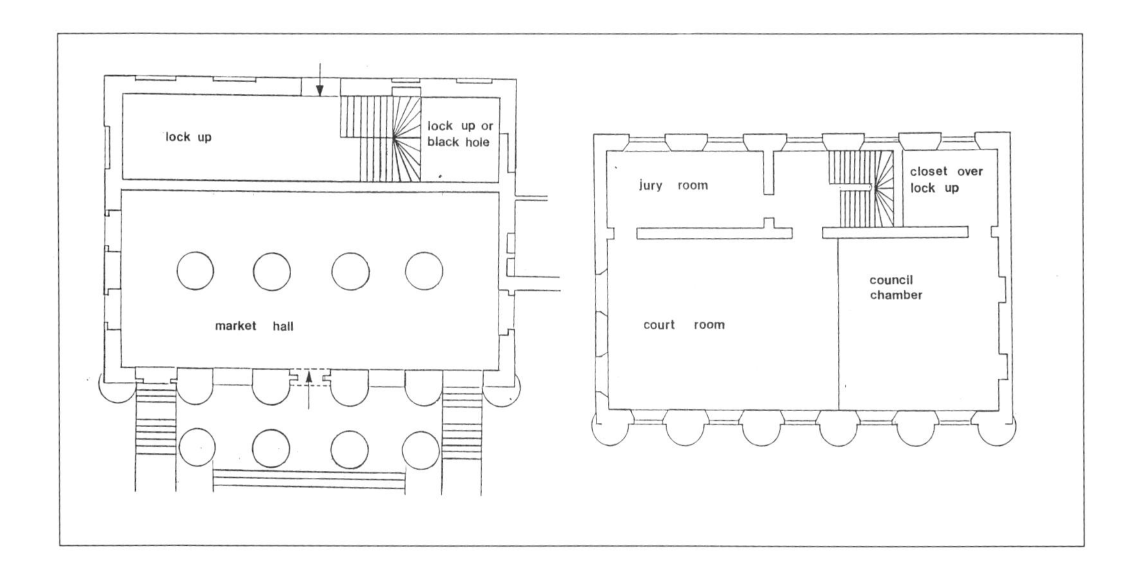

Above:
Plan of the old Town Hall as it was before the Victorian alterations, from a sketch by J. S. Slinger. The ground floor formed a Corn Exchange and was open to the elements at the front, being closed by iron gates at night. Cellars below the building, accessible by outside stairs, were let out as shops.

Below:
'Lancaster Sessions House and Market' (alias the old Town Hall) engraved after Westall, 1829. The building is shown in its original form, with urns on the roof and an open ground floor with iron railings. Later blackening of the stonework has obscured the garlands and swags on Thomas Harrison's cupola.

The former St.Anne's church, Moor Lane, now the Duke's Theatre, was built in 1796. The fenestration shows that like most churches of its period it had a gallery extending around three sides, providing the maximum seating in the smallest space. There was considerable convergence between the roles of theatre and church.

elevation to St. Anne's Place is more complex. There are five windows, the second and fourth having small pediments over them. These windows were originally doors. Above these are five lunette windows, the central one having a pediment over it, and in the roof space two smaller windows. Bellcote at west end. The east end originally terminated in a small apse.

Moor Lane Mills (North and South)

The history of these mills is very complex. North Mill of six storeys, built *c.*1819. South Mill included early buildings, now demolished. Present buildings include six storey L-shaped spinning mill of *c.*1825–31. North Mill is probably on the site of Mr Hadwen's sailcloth factory dating from before 1794.[82]

New Street

New Street contains a number of houses now mostly converted to shops which must date from soon after its creation in 1745. Window surrounds are usually of massive plain stones, typical of more modest buildings in Lancaster of the first half of the 18th century. Two of the frontages have been converted from warehouses, the traditional vertical loading slots becoming windows.

Children's Library

Built in 1823 as the Savings Bank and remodelled by Edward Paley in 1848. The Bank closed in 1889 and in 1931 was adapted to serve as the new

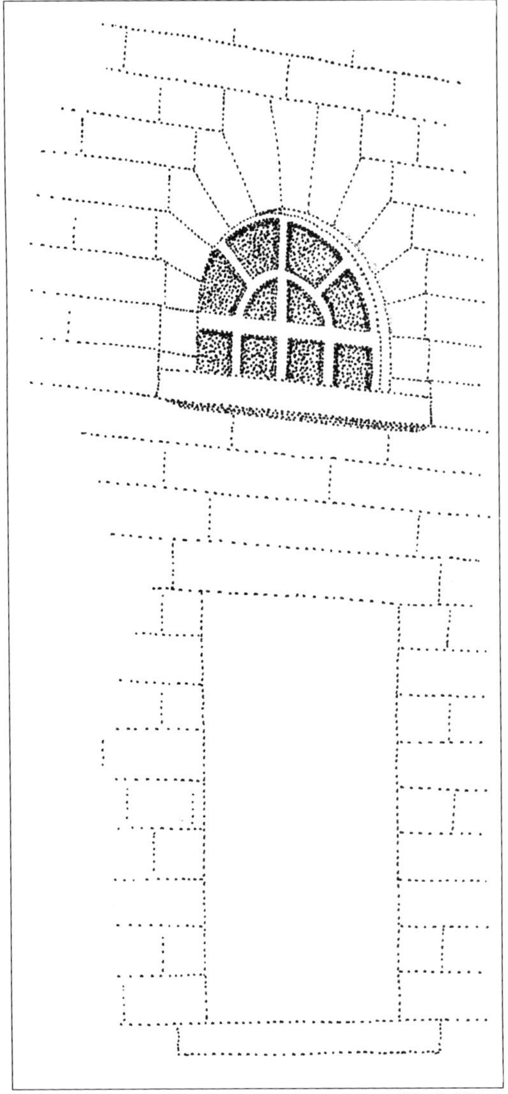

Wendy Moore

Lunette window (on former St. Anne's Church.)

Children's Library. The frontage is Greek Revival with fluted Ionic columns. The architect is unknown, but may have been William Coulthart.

QUEEN'S SQUARE

Falcon House

Three buildings, of which the centre part is of four bays x three storeys. In the central pediment, in order to pull the composition together, is a large Diocletian window set over four windows, something of a solecism; the Classical ideal would be three. The clutter of square and canted bay windows represents Victorian additions. The house to the left of the frontage, built for Mr. Bowes, was cut back to allow street widening in 1937.

Several of the shops in New Street were formerly warehouses as is clear from the blocked or glazed loading slots and corbels for temporary footboards. Georgian Lancaster never became so grand that it turned its back on the trade that made its merchants rich.

No. 1

A house of five bays x two storeys, built before 1778. Very plain with chinese chippendale pattern in the glazing bars of the window over the door. Lancaster Moor stone with its iron patterning can be seen here to good effect. In 1973 the facade of this house was taken down, every stone numbered, and rebuilt.

Queen Street

No. 4
A building of five bays x two storeys, built before 1778. Main door approached by flight of steps. Small extension to left hand side with a projecting canted bay.

Nos. 5 & 7
A pair of large houses with matching swan's neck pediments over the doors. What a pity that the two are not decorated to match! Each house is of three bays x four storeys plus a heavily rusticated basement storey. Main doors set at first floor level with steps and railings. Remains of lampstand outside the door. Built after 1778 (they do not appear on Mackreth's map).[83]

Nos. 19 & 20
A pair of houses of two bays each x three storeys. Doors with fanlights paired centrally under simple porch. These houses stand oddly alone, as though part of a speculative development which was never completed.

St. George's Quay

Lancaster's first purpose-built Quay dates from 1750–55, followed in 1767 by New Quay, used occasionally by Brockbanks the shipbuilders for launching their larger vessels; Ford Quay came later. St. George's Quay is lined with warehouses, pubs, and houses, resulting mainly from three sales of building lots between 1750 and 1780, of which the following are a small sample. The earliest derricks are of timber, with a movable arm; later come fixed beams with pulleys over the centre of the loading doors, and later still are derricks of metal. None of the warehouses is fireproofed, the floors being supported by massive beams.

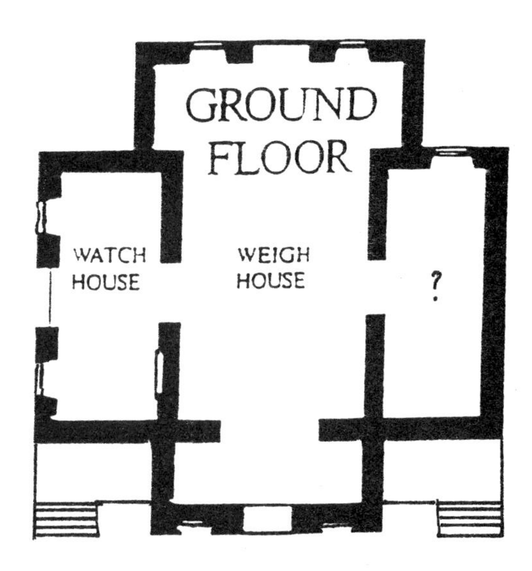

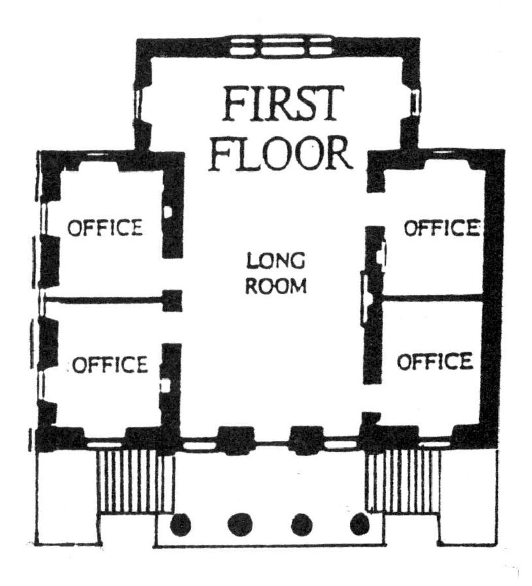

Plan showing the original layout of the Custom House. On the upper floor the Long Room, where initial contact was made, was flanked by offices. The ground floor was used for storage, weighing of goods, and as a depot for the Searcher's boat crew, who had to be ready to intercept vessels entering the port at any time of day or night.

Victoria Court
The former Victoria Corn Mill, converted into housing. A typical warehouse of four storeys with cargo-handling doors running vertically up the centre and a derrick for hoisting at the top.

(West of Pine Street)
Two relatively unrestored warehouses, both of four storeys with centrally-placed loading doors and derricks.

(Adjacent to Duke Street)
Another four storey warehouse with centrally placed timber doors, flanked by windows and with a metal derrick.

No. 23
An unusual house of two bays x three storeys with a door offset to the right. The whole building had settled during the course of building and the left hand side is considerably lower than the right. Plain window surrounds but elaborate quoins at the corners.

No. 25
A house of three bays x three storeys, the door offset to the left. Plain solid window surrounds of the 1750s.

The Custom House
Since 1985 the home of Lancaster Maritime Museum. A Palladian building of two storeys with the entrance at first floor level by two flights of steps returning over a rusticated basement. Windows have alternately round-and triangular-headed pediments. To the front is an Ionic tetrastyle (four-columned) portico with a pediment. The front is ashlar faced, but the sides and rear are of coursed rubble or rendered. The rear of the Long Room is lit by a large Venetian window. Designed by Richard Gillow and built 1762–4.

No. 26
Three warehouses under two roofs with five levels of loading doors flanked by square windows and a blank lunette in the gable of the larger building. One of them was built by Mr. Satterthwaite, merchant, of Castle Park. Timber derricks to the two upper loading bays. The entire eastern wall was replaced in 1984.

No. 35
Warehouse of five storeys, with timber loading doors and flanking windows, now derelict. Adjacent to this to the right another warehouse of three storeys of similar design and remains of another to the right of this again also of three storeys, with a timber derrick.

Wendy Moore
Venetian window (on Custom House, St. George's Quay.)

Between Nos. 26 & 35 a range of simple houses with plain window surrounds mostly of the mid-18th century.

St. Leonardgate

Grand Theatre
Original theatre of 1782, built by subscription under the direction of Messrs. Austin & Whitlock, who managed a circuit of theatres including Whitehaven, Sheffield, Manchester, Newcastle and Chester. Four bays x three storeys with various modern extensions and alterations including a fly tower. The original interior was destroyed in a fire in 1908. The facade below the cornice is original except for the doorways at the extreme right and left.[84]

Nos. 108 & 110
A pair of houses of three bays each x three

The Theatre, built by subscription and finished in 1782, stands in St. Leonardgate. Like most old theatres it has not survived unscathed, the interior having been burnt out in 1908, after this photograph was taken. The facade was later altered with a new door to the pit on the left; the fly tower at the rear was a late 19th century addition.

storeys, the two doorways being brought together under one pediment in the centre, with plain Doric capitals. Built before 1778; no. 108 was acquired in 1792 by James Booth, Collector of Customs for the port, according to the deeds.[85]

Rhodes House, Nos. 112 & 114

Another pair of houses of three bays each x three storeys but this time the central two bays project slightly and carry a pediment. Built before 1778. The doorways, with Doric doorcases, are set at either end, each approached by a small flight of steps.

The Tramway Hotel

Former house of five bays x three storeys, very plain.

SUN STREET

Music Room

A garden building or summer house dating from the 1730s, in the form of a Roman triumphal arch. It was already out of use by 1797, when the gardens in which it stood were sold for building. Three storeys, with Ionic pilasters, the main first floor window with a broken pediment. Balustraded parapet along the top. Inside, the first floor has elaborate plaster work depicting the nine muses and early Roman emperors, probably by itinerant Italian plasterers. Similar work can be found at Towneley Hall and Burrow Hall, both in Lancashire. The arch of the ground floor is now glazed, but would once have formed an arbour.

The Lune Aqueduct carrying the Lancaster Canal over the river, upstream of Lancaster. Built by Rennie and Stevens it was opened in 1797 and immediately became something of a tourist attraction. Its vast cost and the technical problems encountered also made certain that the canal would never be finished in the manner intended.

Nos. 25 & 27

This building has two large arched entrances which presumably once served as stables or carriages houses for adjacent buildings, with accommodation over. Built after 1797, and served as the town's Police Station until 1874.

Nos. 28 & 29

A pair of houses under one roof. Four bays x four storeys. The second bay from the left is shared between the two buildings and the doorways are paired under a single pediment. An additional bay at the right hand end over-rides a carriage entrance. Built soon after 1797.

Water Street

No. 1

House of five bays x three storeys with a basement. Venetian door, centrally placed, approached by steps. Central upper windows both tripartite. Side elevation to Cable Street of three bays x three storeys. This house figures prominently in J. C. Ibbetson's 1798 painting of Cable Street, which shows it, however, with Venetian windows on the upper floors.

Outlying Buildings

Aqueduct Bridge, Caton Road

A bridge of five arches carrying the Lancaster Canal over the river Lune. Turned balusters and a cartouche carrying an inscription on either elevation. Designed by Alexander Stevens and John Rennie and opened 1797 at a cost of £48,000. This aqueduct became a tourist attraction from the moment it was opened. Alexander Stevens did not live to see his work complete; the parish registers record the burial of 'Alexander Stevens – Aqueduct Bridge Architect from Scotland' on 4th January, 1796.[86] A monument to him can be seen on the outer south wall of the Priory church.

Bath House, Bath Street

An outwardly anonymous stone building of two bays x two storeys fronting onto Bath Street, this Bath House was built in 1803 by subscription, and designed by J. M. Gandy.[87] The only indications of its function is the row of chimneys at the rear of the building presumably connected with heating the water.

Skerton Bridge

Of five semi-elliptical arches and with a flat deck throughout. Pierced turned balustrading and aedicules between each of the arches. Designed by Thomas Harrison 1783, and built 1783–8. Harrison won the competition for its design and this brought him to Lancaster. The bridge allowed a new and grander entry to the town than its medieval predecessor downstream.

Wendy Moore

Aedicule (on Skerton Bridge.)

Bridge Houses, Parliament Street

A group of three buildings. In the centre a house of three bays x two storeys, the upper floor level marked by paired engaged Ionic columns, four pairs in all. Entrance centrally placed with a pediment over it. On either side are screen walls of alternating round-and square-headed niches (three round, two square to either side) ending in a pavilion, of three bays x two storeys with a blank central window on the upper floor. Over the centre bay of the centre building is a cartouche for an inscription which appears never to have been used. At the rear the apparent organisation of the front is belied by the much more random layout of buildings. A long stair window can be seen at the rear of the centre building. The main building served as a toll-house for this new approach to Lancaster over Skerton Bridge. Thomas Harrison seems to have been responsible for the design of this as well as of the bridge.[88]

Lancaster Moor Hospital

Formerly the County Lunatic Asylum. The oldest building dates from 1811–1816 and was designed by Thomas Standen (or Stanton) of Lancaster. It is of five bays x three storeys with a giant Tuscan pediment to the front carried on four engaged columns. The lower storey is rusticated, and there are two wings. The whole effect must originally have been that of a country house, set in its own grounds. Despite the institutional surroundings something of this effect survives. Heating of rooms was by hot water, thus avoiding the risks caused to the patients by open fires.

Penny Street Station

Although it dates from 1839–40 the former railway terminus of the Lancaster & Preston Junction Railway, designed by Edwin Gwyther of Birmingham, is purely Georgian in style and tries to look like a private villa. Perhaps this is because a grammar of architecture for railway stations had not yet become established. The front contained the main entrance and offices while the back opened onto platforms. Now it forms part of a Nurse's Home and offices for the Hospital and Health Authority.

The central block forming the oldest part of the Lancaster Moor Hospital, originally the County Lunatic Asylum. Finished in 1816 it was designed by Thomas Standen and takes the external form of a country house.

Engraving of the New Bridge, now known as Skerton Bridge, by Landseer after Farington, 1791. Many artists, including Turner, were attracted to sketch this beautiful bridge from the same viewpoint.

White Cross Mill
Recent demolition has exposed what seems to be part of the earliest building of *c.*1802 at the centre of the complex, which has survived all the vicissitudes of the mill. It is a rectangular stone multi-floored block, the upper storeys of which have been rebuilt.[89]

SKERTON

Across the river from Lancaster itself Skerton was for centuries a separate village. In the late 18th and early 19th century a number of gentlemens' villas were built here in what were then still rural surroundings. These included Lune Bank, Lune Villa and Ryelands House.

Ryelands House
Built in 1836 for Jonathan Dunn, retired carriage-builder and twice mayor of Lancaster, it is still Georgian in character. The main block, of stone, is of five x three bays and two storeys. A large extension with a tower was added in 1883 by Paley & Austin for Lord Ashton.

South of the town development was very sporadic and had to wait until the middle of the 19th century. Hardly any buildings stood between Penny Street and Scotforth, which was then a separate village. Among the few houses were Springfield Hall, a house of *c.*1790, its site now occupied by the Hospital, and Bowerham House, which still stands, an ancient manorial site.

This is by no means an exhaustive list of Georgian buildings in Lancaster but I hope that the list includes the most interesting examples.

Notes

1. Descriptions and illustrations of some building are to be found in: N. Pevsner, *The Buildings of England; North Lancashire*, 1969; 'Prospect of Lancaster', *Architects' Journal*, 1972; D. Cruickshank, *A Guide to the Georgian Buildings of Britain and Ireland*, 1985; J. Champness, *Lancashire's Architectural Heritage*, 1989.
2. A. Whincop & A. White, *Lancaster's Maritime Heritage*, 1986, 6–32.
3. G. Lindop (ed.), *T. de Quincey, Confessions of an English Opium Eater & Other Writings*, 1985, 217.
4. Sir G. Head, *A Home Tour through the Manufacturing Districts of England in the Summer of 1835*, 2nd. ed., 1968, 429.
5. J. W. A. Price, *Industrial Archaeology of the Lune Valley*, University of Lancaster, Occasional Papers no. 13, 1983, 30–37.
6. M. M. Schofield, *Outlines of an Economic History of Lancaster, 1680–1860*, pt. 2, 1951, 123–4.
7. P. Mulholland, 'The Origin of St. George's Quay, Lancaster and the warehouse No. 35 St. George's Quay' (unpublished, University of Lancaster, North West Regional Studies Centre).
8. Notts. Record Office, M380
9. A. J. White, 'Damasgill or Mainstones Quarry, Ellel', *Contrebis* XIII, 1986–7, 20–21.
10. 'Beauties of the North: Lancaster' *The Lonsdale Magazine*, 1, 1820, 469 (repr. 1989)
11. D. Ross & A. J. White, *The Lancaster Custom House*, Lancaster City Museums Local Studies no. 9, 1988.
12. R. Bellis & G. M. Shackleton, 'Slate Delfes in Quarmor', *Contrebis*, 8, 1980, 53–6.
13. Ross & White, *op. cit.*
14. Lancashire Record Office, MBLa, Box 82
15. E. Baines, *History, Directory & Gazetteer of the County Palatine of Lancaster, 1825*, vol. 2, 2
16. D. Cruickshank & N. Burton, *Life in the Georgian City*, 1990, 104–15.
17. Custom House, see Ross & White, *op. cit.*; Town Hall, Lancaster Borough Records, Bailiffs' Book H, 1772–1796, ff. 187–92; Assembly Room, Lancaster Central Library, MS 118.
18. Lancaster Central Library, MSS 2335–8.
19. A. Clifton Taylor & A. S. Ireson, *English Stone Buildings*, 1983, 174; for Alexander Stevens jnr. see *Lancaster Guardian* 23/8/1856 p. 4, c. 6.
20. J. Champness, 'The Architecture of Richard Gillow, 1734–1811', unpublished dissertation, Liverpool Polytechnic School of Planning.
21. *Thomas Harrison in Lancaster*, Visual Arts Centre, University of Lancaster, 1978; *The Order of the Day; Thomas Harrison 1744–1829 and Architecture of the Greek Revival*, Whitworth Art Gallery, nd; *The Modest Genius: An Exhibition of Drawings and Works of Thomas Harrison*, Grosvenor Museum, Chester, 1977.
22. W. O. Roper (ed.), *Materials for the History of the Church of Lancaster, III*, Chetham Society vol. 58, 1906, 626–32
23. *Army List*, 1782, 18.
24. Cruickshank, 1985, *op. cit.*, 114.
25. Lancaster City Museum, LM 74.69/1
26. Lancaster Central Library, MS 3706
27. B. Tyson, 'Some Harbour works in West Cumberland before 1700', *Transactions of the Ancient Monuments Society*, 29, 1985, 180ff, 201–4.
28. J. D. Marshall (ed.), *The Autobiography of William Stout of Lancaster, 1665–1752*, 1967, 226.
29. Lancaster Central Library, MS 3706
30. Lancashire Record Office, MBLa, Box 82
31. Lancaster Borough Records, Bailiffs' Book H, 1772–1796, ff. 187–92
32. Lancashire Record Office, QAR 2/5 (1783).
33. C. Clark, *An Historical and Descriptive Account of the Town of Lancaster*, 1807, 23.
34. Lancaster Borough Records, Bailiffs' Accounts, Rentals, Book F, 1736–71, f. 203; Orders, Elections etc., Book Ka, 1756–94, f2
35. Lancaster Central Library, PL 1/50
36. A. J. White, 'Stone-Masons in a Georgian Town', *The Local Historian*, 21, no. 2, 1991, 60–65
37. J. Summerson, *The Classical Language of Architecture*, 1980
38. Cruickshank, 1985, *op. cit.*
39. J. Summerson, *The Architecture of the Eighteenth Century*, 1986; J. Summerson, *Georgian London*, 1978; W. Ison, *The Georgian Buildings of Bath 1700–1830*, 1980.
40. Cruickshank & Burton, 1990, *op. cit.*, 197
41. Cross-Fleury, *Time-Honoured Lancaster*, 1891, 448
42. J. M. Robinson, *A Guide to the Country Houses of the North West*, 1988, 169–70, 246–7
43. W. Stukeley, *Itinerarium Curiosum*, 1776 (1724 data), II, 38
44. D. Butler, *Summer Houses of Kendal*, Abbot Hall,

1982
45. Lancaster City Museum, LM 70.17
46. Cross-Fleury, *op. cit.*, 1891, 443–6
47. K. H. Docton, *A Directory of Lancaster 1766*, 1958; Lancashire Record Office, DDCa
48. M. Elder, *Lancaster and the African Slave Trade*, Lancaster City Museums Local Studies, no. 14, 1991
49. C. Dickens, 'The Lazy Tour of Two Idle Apprentices', *Household Words*, no. 395, Oct. 1857
50. Marshall (ed.), *op. cit.*, 96 (sd 1689); see also S. & N. Buck's engraving entitled 'A North-East Prospect of Lancaster', 1728, which shows the Green Ayre in the foreground.
51. Lancaster Borough Records, Book C, Old Constitutions, Orders etc., 1679–1736, ff 23–5, 34, 43–4, 50–1, 56, 59; Lancaster Central Library, MS 208 f. 46ff.
52. T. Cann Hughes, *Notes on the County Town of Lancaster in the 18th Century*, 1935, 20, 22.
53. Act of Parliament 1749, 'An Act for improving the Navigation of the River Loyne, otherwise called Lune: and for building a Quay or Wharf near the Town of Lancaster in the County Palatine of Lancaster'.
54. Lancaster Central Library, Port Commission Records
55. Plan in Lancaster City Museum. See also Lancaster Borough Records, Minute Book 1756–94, 230ff.
56. *Ibid.*, 264–5.
57. Lancaster City Museum, LMA 287
58. Lancaster Borough Records, Minute Book 1756–94, 238–9.
59. Act of Parliament, 1784, 'An Act to explain and amend a Power vested in John Dalton, Esquire, to grant Leases, so far as it concerns certain Lands and Hereditaments within the Town or Precincts of Lancaster, called The Fryerage, and for the other purposes therein mentioned'.
60. Lancaster Central Library, MS 1532.
61. Information from deeds in possession of Mr. D. Atkinson, Dalton Square, to whom I am most grateful.
62. *Ibid.*
63. Lancaster City Council, Deeds.
64. J. Fox, 'High Street House, Lancaster', *Contrebis*, 8, 1980, 42–52
65. Lancaster Central Library, PL 1/108.
66. G. Fandrey, *The Craggs of Greenbank*, nd, *sub* 1799.
67. Lancaster Central Library, Pamphlet Box S10
68. *Ibid.*
69. Lancaster Central Library, MS 4479; Lancashire Record Office also has a rough undated plan of the same development, with a few small differences, in DDMa 25.
70. *The Landmark Handbook*, 1977, 82–5.
71. Champness, dissertation.
72. Clark, *op. cit.*, 20–29; watercolours by J. Freebairn in Lancaster City Museum show the Castle before and after the earliest round of improvements.
73. Roper, *op. cit.*, 624.
74. *Cumberland Pacquet*, 22/4/1783.
75. Cruickshank, *op. cit.*, 220.
76. see M. Lort, *Archaeologia*, V, 1779, 98–100 for a description of Roman remains found during building work here.
77. Lancaster Central Library, MSS 2335–8.
78. K. Docton, 'No.5 Dalton Square', *On Lancaster*, 1971.
79. Binns' map, 1821 (that is the date printed on the map but it would appear to have actually been published some three years later).
80. Fox, *loc. cit.*
81. E. Kennerley, *William Penny and Penny's Almshouses*, Lancaster City Museums Local Studies, no. 3.
82. Lancaster Central Library, PL 2/14, plan dated 1819.
83. K. Downes, *The Georgian Cities of Britain*, 1979, 36.
84. A. Betjeman, *The Grand Theatre, Lancaster; Two Centuries of Entertainment*, University of Lancaster, Occasional Paper no. 11, 1982.
85. Lancaster City Council, Deeds, 194/6.
86. Lancashire Record Office, Lancaster Parish Registers.
87. H. M. Colvin, *Biographical Dictionary of British Architects 1600–1840*, 1978, 328–9.
88. Lancaster Borough Records, Minute Book 1756–1794, ff. 264–5.
89. J. Price, *Industrial Lancaster*, Lancaster City Museums Local Studies no. 12, 1989.

Occasional Papers from the Centre for North-West Regional Studies

Flowering Plants and Ferns of Cumbria	G. Halliday	£2.95
Early Lancaster Friends	M. Mullet	£2.95
North-West Theses and Dissertations, 1950–78	U. Lawler	£6.00
Lancaster: The Evolution of its Townscape to 1800	S. Penney	£2.95
Richard Marsden and the Preston Chartists, 1837–48	J. King	£2.95
The Grand Theatre, Lancaster	A. Betjemann	£2.95
Popular Leisure and the Music Hall in 19th-century Bolton	R. Poole	£2.95
Industrial Archaeology of the Lune Valley	J. Price	£2.95
The Diary of William Fisher of Barrow, 1811–59	W. Rollinson/B. Harrison	£2.95
Rural Life in South-West Lancashire, 1840–1914	A. Mutch	£3.95
Grand Fashionable Nights: Kendal Theatre, 1575–1985	M. Eddershaw	£3.95
The Roman Fort and Town of Lancaster	D. Shotter/A. White	£4.95
Windermere in the nineteenth century	O. M. Westall	£4.95
A Traditional Grocer: T. D. Smith's of Lancaster	M. Winstanley	£4.95
Reginald Farrer: Dalesman, Planthunter, Gardener	J. Illingworth/J. Routh	£4.95
Walking Roman Roads in Bowland	P. Graystone	£4.95
The Royal Albert: Chronicles of an Era	J. Alston	£4.95
From Lancaster to the Lakes – The Region in Literature	K. Hanley/A. Milbank	£5.95

Each of these titles may be ordered by post from:

C.N.W.R.S.,
Fylde College,
University of Lancaster,
Bailrigg, Lancaster

Books will be despatched post free to UK addresees.
Please make cheques payable to 'The University of Lancaster'.
Titles are also available from all good booksellers within the region.